A Primer on the Empowering
Work of the Holy Spirit

Although "primer" (pri-mer) and "primer" (prim-er)
are spelled the same,
one is a paint and the other
a small, introductory book on a subject.

Philip J. Noordmans

A Primer on the Empowering Work of the Holy Spirit

ISBN-13: 978-1985765245
ISBN-10: 1981954376

This book has not been professionally edited. Hence, you may find typos, etc.

Author: Philip J. Noordmans
Publisher: Kindle Direct Publishing

Front cover photo by "not brittany shh pls" on Unsplash. Narracan Falls, Narracan, Australia.

Back cover photo by Philip J. Noordmans.

With deep appreciation to the team of coworkers whom God
has used and is using to nurture my understanding and practice
regarding the Person and work of the Holy Spirit.

Thank you also to the individuals who contributed stories
to this collective effort to pass on a balanced theological
and experiential understanding
of the empowering work of Holy Spirit.

Table of Contents

1. A Surprising Discovery

"My wrist really hurts," said Gabrielle, "and I'm not sure why. Maybe it is arthritis or something like that." Her small circle of friends listened sympathetically unsure of how to respond. It was obvious that she was struggling to hold back the tears. Eventually Emma said to the group, "Maybe we should pray for her." Heads nodded in agreement but no one moved. Then Emma turned to Edward. "I think you are supposed to pray for Gabrielle's wrist."

"What, me?" replied Edward.

Doubts and fears jostled within 20-year old Edward's mind. Two weeks earlier the group had prayed for him and the Spirit of God had worked through their prayers to bring deep repentance and a measure of deliverance. Edward knew that God was radically changing his life for good, but the thought of stepping out to pray for healing for Gabrielle felt like a huge risk. "What if I pray and nothing happens?" he said to himself. Nevertheless, he sensed the Holy Spirit's nudge to take a step of faith and pray. The groups joined Edward in surrounding Gabrielle. Before they prayed, Edward asked, "On a scale of one to ten, what level of pain are you feeling?"

"Seven, maybe eight," replied Gabrielle.

"May I put my hand on your wrist as we pray?" asked Edward.

"Sure, of course."

Timidly, awkwardly, Edward began. "Pain, in the Name of Jesus, be gone! Wrist, in the Name of Jesus, be healed and be restored!"

Unsure of what to say next, he simply waited. In time he asked, "What level of pain are you feeling now?"

Gabrielle moved her wrist and exclaimed with glowing joy, "The pain is gone! It is all gone!"

That evening Edward discovered that Jesus is real and that the Holy Spirit is willing and able to empower ordinary people to cooperate with Him to do Kingdom work.

2. Jesus, a Spirit Empowered Man

If you would have asked me [Phil] prior to the year 2000 why Jesus was able to teach with authority, open blind eyes, and drive out evil spirits, I would have replied, "Because He was God, and God can do anything He wants." My follow-up statement would have been, "But I am not God, so please do not expect me to do any of those things."

In due time God brought a much-needed corrective to my perspective.

While attending a Dunamis Fellowship event in Black Mountain, North Carolina, in the year 2000, Tom asked me a question that led to deeper-level change in my approach to ministry. He introduced his question by pointing to a familiar text. "Scripture states in Philippians 2," Tom noted, "that Jesus,

> *though he was in the form of God, did not count equality with God a thing to be grasped, but emptied*

himself, by taking the form of a servant, being born in the likeness of men. Philippians 2:6-7, ESV

Then came Tom's penetrating question. "Of what did Jesus empty Himself?"

Yes, I know that scholars had been wrestling with that question for centuries. Further, one of my first assignments in a theology class at Fuller Theological Seminary was to exegete that text. However, due to the Holy Spirit's work in my mind and heart at that time, Tom's question carried fresh significance.

Of What Did Jesus Empty Himself?

In a word, Jesus emptied Himself of His right to function as God while on earth. Jesus let go of His divine prerogatives and choose to live His life as a man among men. Jesus did not cease being God; rather, He added full humanity to His full deity.

- The ESV Study Bible states that "The 'emptying' consisted of his becoming human, not of his giving up any part of His true deity."[1]

- Dr. John Walvoord observed, "Christ did not empty Himself of deity, but of its outward manifestation. He emptied Himself by taking the form of a servant. ... The incarnation did not change the person and attributes of Christ in His divine nature, but added to it a complete human nature. ... Christ voluntarily, moment by moment, submitted to human limitations apart from sin.[2]

Although Jesus was fully God and fully man, while on earth He chose to voluntarily limit the use of His divine attributes. He

---

[1] ESVSB (English Standard Version Study Bible), (Wheaton, IL: Crossway Bible, 2008), 2283.

[2] John Walvoord, "Philippians 2: *At The Name Of Jesus Every Knee Should Bow.*" http://preceptaustin.org/philippians_25-11.htm#2:7

functioned as a man among men but without sin. Renowned
Bible scholar R.C. Sproul stated plainly,

> The idea that Jesus' two natures were like alternating
> electrical circuits, so that sometimes He acted in His
> humanity and sometimes in His Divinity, is also
> mistaken.[3]

Profound Implications for Ministry

I have come to understand that while He was on earth, Jesus
functioned as a Holy Spirit empowered man. At His baptism,
the Holy Spirit descended "upon" Him equipping Him to
minister with power and authority. Jesus Himself explained His
consciousness of the Holy Spirit's power surging through Him
to speak anointed words and to do might works when He
declared,

> But if it is by the Spirit of God that I cast out demons,
> then the Kingdom of God has come upon you. Matthew
> 12:28, ESV[4]

The Apostle Peter witnessed to the Holy Spirit's work through
Jesus when he wrote,

> God anointed Jesus of Nazareth with the Holy Spirit
> and with power. He went about doing good and healing
> all who were oppressed by the devil, for God was with
> him, Acts 10:38, ESV

Here's the point. Since the Holy Spirit, who rested upon Jesus
and empowered Him to speak anointed words and do mighty
works, is also available to us, we, too, may be equipped to
speak prophetically, teach with authority, heal the sick, and

---

[3] R.C. Sproul, General Editor, *Reformation Study Bible* (Orlando, FL:
Ligonier Ministries, 2005), 1836.
[4] In many instances throughout this Primer, underlining, bold, and italics
have been added by PJN for emphasis.

cast out evil spirits. We, too, may live, love, and serve in the Spirit's power.

However, Spirit-empowered living does not happen automatically. Just as Jesus' baptism with the Holy Spirit proved to be a dynamic turning point in His life, so our lives will be deeply changed when we experience the baptism with the Holy Spirit.

Because this concept is so important to living a balanced, Spirit-filled life, let's slow down and take a closer look.

3. Jesus' Baptism: A Dynamic Turning Point

Prior to His baptism,[5] there is no record of Jesus teaching,[6] preaching, performing miracles or casting out evil spirits. Based on the gospel's record, however, we can say with confidence that following His baptism in water and with the Holy Spirit, a major shift occurred. The Holy Spirit descended upon Him (Luke 3:21-22) and He went forth in the power of the Spirit (Luke 4:14) to preach, teach, and do miracles.

In a similar way a significant shift will occur in our lives when we invite Jesus to baptize us with the Holy Spirit.

- Prior to our baptism with the Holy Spirit, the Holy Spirit works in us to sanctify us, that is, to transform us little by little into Christ-like servants by growing the fruit of the Spirit in us.

- A turning point occurs when we humbly, sincerely, and in faith ask Jesus to baptize us with the Holy Spirit.

---

[5] Matthew 3:13-17; Mark 1:9-11; Luke 3:21-22; John 1:29-34.
[6] Implied exception: Jesus, age 12, Luke 2:41-50.

o Prior to our baptism with the Spirit, we exercise some of the functional gifts of the Spirit (Romans 12:1-8) and see much fruit result from abiding in Christ (John 15:1-17).

o After our baptism with the Spirit, Jesus adds to our functional gifts *the manifestations of the Spirit for the common good* (1 Corinthians 12:7) and we are equipped, as Jesus was, to go forth in the Holy Spirit's power (Luke 4:14) to preach, teach, disciple, prophesy, speak words of wisdom, heal the sick, and drive out evil spirits.

Listen closely to a few observations from the lips of renowned Biblical scholars.

- Reformed Theologian R.C. Sproul

  "Jesus has the divine nature from the moment of His conception all the way till now and on to eternity. So what is the significance of the Holy Spirit coming upon Him? It is the Holy Spirit anointing the human nature of Jesus. We tend to think that the miracles that Jesus performed He performed in His divine nature. No! He performed them in His human nature through the power of the Holy Spirit that was given to Him at His baptism. Here [at His baptism] is where God is empowering Jesus to fulfill the mission that He has."[7]

- Talbot Theology professor J.P. Moreland

  "When I was saved in the late 1960s, I was taught that Jesus' miracles proved he was God because he did them from His divine nature. It has become clear to me, however, that this was wrong, for Jesus' public ministry was done as He, a perfect man, did what he saw his

---

[7] R.C. Sproul, sermon, "Baptism & Temptation of Jesus." Ligonier Ministries: Message of the Month, February 2014.

Father doing in dependence on the filling of the Holy Spirit."[8]

- Dallas Seminary professor Dr. Thomas Constable

"Luke viewed the power of God as extrinsic[9] to Jesus (cf. John 5:1-19). Jesus did not perform miracles out of His divine nature. He laid those powers aside at the Incarnation. Rather, He did His miracles in the power of God's Spirit—who was on Him and in Him—as a prophet. … In Acts, Luke would stress that the same Spirit is on and in every believer today, and He is the source of our power as He was the source of Jesus' power."[10]

The same Holy Spirit who empowered Jesus' life and ministry lives in us from the moment of our conversion. Following our baptism with the Holy Spirit, he also comes "upon" us on an as-needed basis to empower us to say words that God wants said and/or to do works that God wants done.

4. Baptism With The Holy Spirit

Bob's Story

I was a youth pastor for a Free Methodist Church in the early 1970s. At that time many in my youth group were going to places and receiving the "baptism" and I was jealous. When I was talking to one of the girls about her experience, she sensed that I was upset even though

---

[8] J. P. Moreland, *Kingdom Triangle* (Grand Rapids: Zondervan, 2007), 174.
[9] Extrinsic: Not part of the essential nature of someone or something; coming or operating from outside. Merriam-Webster Dictionary online.
[10] Dr. Thomas Constable, in his Commentary on Luke 5:17. We will point out that the Spirit is not automatically "on" every believer.

I was trying to hide my true feelings. When she confronted me, I then admitted that I was frustrated that kids in my youth group were having spiritual experiences and I wasn't.

We agreed to meet on a Tuesday night at a local community college where she was attending. As we sat there talking, she simply said for me to start praying. After a while I felt like a wind (not physical, but supernatural) starting above me and then settling inside me. I wasn't saying anything to her as to what was going on. She suddenly shouted out "don't think in English!" I then opened my mouth and began speaking what I am convinced was Mandarin Chinese. I can't prove that but I believe it with all my soul. I kept speaking for a long time and eventually went home ecstatic.

When I (Phil) began hanging around Charismatics, I heard them talking about being "baptized with the Holy Spirit." That phrase puzzled me. I thought, "What do they mean?" And, what difference does it make?" My objective in this chapter is not only to clarify the Biblical meaning of the phrase "baptism with the Holy Spirit" but also to begin to create a thirst within us to experience it. John the Baptist declared,

> *"I baptize you with water for repentance, but he who is coming after me is mightier than I, whose sandals I am not worthy to carry. He will baptize you with the Holy Spirit and fire." Matthew 3:11, ESV*

Just before His ascension, Jesus himself spoke about this "baptism with the Holy Spirit" when He said to His disciples,

> *John baptized with water, but you will be baptized with the Holy Spirit not many days from now. Acts 1:5, ESV*

I expect that the disciples wondered, "What does that mean? And, when will it happen?" Jesus proceeded,

> *You will receive power when the Holy Spirit has come* *upon you, and you will be my witnesses in Jerusalem and in all Judea and Samaria, and to the end of the earth. Acts 1:8, ESV*

When the distinction registered in my heart and mind between the Holy Spirit dwelling "in" every true believer, and the Holy Spirit coming "upon" us, it rocked my world. I came to see that Scripture teaches two Spirit baptisms.

A. Two Spirit Baptisms

1. Baptism <u>by</u> the Holy Spirit
2. Baptism <u>with</u> the Holy Spirit

Baptism *BY* the Holy Spirit	Baptism *WITH* the Holy Spirit
1 Corinthians 12:13[11]	Acts 1:5, 8; 2:1-4
By the Holy Spirit	By Jesus
Plunged into the Body of Christ	Empowered to witness and serve
When? At the moment of our conversion	When? At the moment of our conversion, or at a later time, i.e., whenever Jesus schedules our "personal Pentecost"

---

[11] For a detailed explanation of this important text, see the chapter in *FireStarter: The Holy Spirit Empowers* entitled "Baptized with the Holy Spirit at Conversion?"

The above understanding fits with I. Howard Marshall's assertion that "baptism" has two basic meanings:[12]

    A. To immerse a person in water [i.e., to plunge a person into water].

Likewise, the Holy Spirit plunges us into the body of Christ.

    B. To deluge a person with water.

Similar concept: Following the victory, the team baptized their coach with Gatorade.

Parallel experience: Standing under a waterfall.

> o This meaning of baptism harmonizes with Jesus' words prior to Pentecost regarding baptism with the Holy Spirit. "*John baptized with water, but you will be baptized with the Holy Spirit not many days from now,*" Acts 1:5, ESV.

Some protest saying that in Ephesians 4:5, Paul teaches that there is only one baptism.

> *There is one body and one Spirit—just as you were called to the one hope that belongs to your call— 5 one Lord, one faith, one baptism, 6 one God and Father of all, who is over all and through all and in all. Ephesians 4:4-6, ESV*

Response:

In Ephesians 4:5, Paul is referring to water baptism and hence, this text does not negate two Spirit-baptisms.

---

[12]I. Howard Marshall, *The Acts of the Apostles* (Grand Rapids, MI: Eerdmans, reprinted 1987).

Some have thought that because Paul says there is one baptism that the idea of the baptism of the Holy Spirit as a subsequent experience is invalid. But Paul only speaks here of the baptism by water which is the visible token of God's common work in every believer, and thus a basis of unity. There aren't separate baptisms for Jew and Gentile.[13]

B. Definitions

A good definition of baptism with the Holy Spirit is simply "power added," and/or "power released."

When Jesus sends the Holy Spirit upon us, He momentarily "ups the voltage" or "activates the turbo-charger" thereby equipping us to advance His agenda in a particular person's life and/or in a specific situation.

- Because the Holy Spirit dwells within ever Christian, we consistently experience a measure of His power and authority.

- When He comes "upon" us, we momentarily experience more, sometimes much more.

This was certainly true for Charles G. Finney (1792-1875). Some historians estimate that during the years 1857-1858, God used Finney directly or indirectly to lead over 100,000 people into a personal relationship with Jesus Christ.

As a young man Finney was a bright law student, proficient in Latin, Greek, and Hebrew. After a struggle with pride, Finney received salvation in the autumn of 1821. A day later, he received a might baptism with the Holy Ghost.

---

[13] David Guzik @ Ephesians 4.
http://www.studylight.org/com/guz/view.cgi?book=eph&chapter=004

Without any expectation of it, without ever having the thought in my mind that there was any such thing for me, without any recollection that I had ever heard the thing mentioned by any person in the world, the Holy ghost descended on me in a manner that seemed to go through me, body and soul. I could feel the impression, like a wave of electricity, going through me. Indeed it seemed to come in waves and waves of liquid love; for I could not express it in any other way. It seemed like the very breath of God. I can recollect distinctly that it seemed to fan me, like immense wings. … I wept aloud with joy and love; and I do not know but I should say, I literally bellowed out the unutterable gushings of my heart. The waves came over me, and over me, one after the other, until I recollect I cried out, "I shall die if these waves continue to pass over me." I said, "Lord, I cannot bear any more;" yet I had no fear of death.[14]

In my reading I have come across several more good definitions of baptism with the Holy Spirit. For example,

John Piper

I think the essence of being baptized with the Holy Spirit is when a person, who is already a believer, receives extraordinary spiritual power for Christ-exalting ministry.[15]

R. A. Torrey

The baptism with the Holy Spirit is a definite experience of which one may and ought to know whether he has received it or not. … a man may be regenerated by the Holy Spirit and still not be baptized with the Holy Spirit. … The baptism with the Holy Spirit is an operation of the Holy

---

[14] J. Gilchrist Lawson, *Deeper Experiences of Famous Christians* (Anderson, IN: The Warner Press, 1911, Second printing July 1972), 180.
[15] http://www.desiringgod.org/library/sermons/90/092390.html

Spirit distinct from and subsequent and additional to His regenerating work.

- In regeneration there is an impartation of life, and the one who receives it is saved;

- In the baptism with the Holy Spirit there is an impartation of power and the one who receives it is fitted for service. ...

In the same context Torrey identified parallel terms used in the New Testament.[16] These include:

- ✓ Baptism with the Holy Spirit
- ✓ Filled with the Holy Spirit
- ✓ The Holy Ghost fell on them
- ✓ The gift of the Holy Ghost was poured out
- ✓ Received the Holy Ghost
- ✓ I send the promise of my Father upon you
- ✓ Endued with power from on high
- ✓ Anointed with power from on high

A person standing on the Canadian side of the Niagara Falls will describe it one way, and a person standing on the American side, another. But it is the same Falls.

A.W. Tozer declared,

> I want here boldly to assert that it is my happy belief that every Christian can have a copious [abundant; plentiful] outpouring of the Holy Spirit in a measure far beyond that received at conversion.[17]

---

[16] Long, Gateways, Revised 2006, page 211, quoting R.A. Torrey, *What the Bible Teaches about the Holy Spirit* (New York: revel, 1898), pp. 270-271.
[17] *Tozer on the Holy Spirit. A 366-day Devotional* Compiled by Marilynne E. Foster, 2007. Entry for November 24.

Illustration: Bob Whitaker's baptism with the Holy Spirit

In his book, *Adventuring with the Holy Spirit*, Bob Whitaker tells about his journey as a Presbyterian pastor in the 1950s and 60s toward experiencing the fullness of the Holy Spirit. First, God used a series of relationships and experiences to warm him up to the things of the Spirit. Then, on October 11, 1962, Bob went to a Thursday morning prayer meeting at the First Assembly of God Church in Phoenix where David duPlessis shared about an Episcopal minister whose life and ministry were transformed by the power of the Holy Spirit.

> As I listened, something was welling up within me. My heart began to pound; it got so loud I though surely the people around me could hear it. I felt like a barrel filled up with pulsating liquid dynamite. I thought "If this keeps up I'm going to burst."

In the middle of duPlessis' talk, Bob raised his hand and said, "I'm sorry to interrupt, but I need you to pray for me right now."[18] David invited Bob forward, laid hands on him, and prayed fervently for him to be released in the Holy Spirit.

> I thought heavens cascading torrents would cause me to speak in tongues, and I was willing, but instead I wept and then peace came over me. David said to me, "Now brother, the Lord is dealing with you. Get alone with Him and your Bible and seek His face and He will meet you."[19]

---

[18] Bob Whitaker, *Adventuring with the Holy Spirit* (Lulu Publishing Services, 2015), 23.

[19] Ibid., 23.

C. Primary Benefit

Acts 1:8 describes the primary benefit that flows into the lives of Christians who experience this "baptism with the Holy Spirit."

> *You will receive power when the Holy Spirit has come upon you, and you will be my witnesses in Jerusalem and in all Judea and Samaria, and to the end of the earth. Acts 1:8, ESV*

Power added.

D. The Gospel's Unstoppable Advance

The promise of Act 1:8 became a reality. Empowered by the Holy Spirit the Apostles and their coworkers carried the gospel from Jerusalem to Judea to Samaria and to the world.

1. Jerusalem -	Acts 1:1 - 6:7
2. Judea and Samaria -	Acts 6:8 - 9:31
3. Gentiles -	Acts 9:32 - 12:25
4. Asia -	Acts 13:1 - 16:5
5. Europe -	Acts 16:6 - 19:20
6. Rome -	Acts 19:21 - 28:31

The Holy Spirit is mission-minded. Each wave of the Spirit pushed the Kingdom of God outward.

One of our tasks is to join the Holy Spirit in advancing the gospel in our Jerusalem and beyond. We will achieve very little without the Holy Spirit's presence and power to propel us forward.

D. L. Moody (1837-1899) stands out as one of the greatest witnesses of all time. In contrast to well-educated Charles Finney, at age seventeen Moody could scarcely read or write. Due to his father's premature death, Moody's family was very poor. Eventually, Moody left home and succeeded as a shoe salesman. In 1854, Moody began attending Mount Vernon Congregational Sunday School and his teacher, Mr. Kimball, led him to Christ. Moody's life changed radically. Before his conversion Moody "worked to be saved; now I work because I am saved."[20]

Moody had a knack for drawing crowds. By age 23, God was using him to touch the lives of thousands of children through his Sunday School efforts in Chicago. Eventually, the parents began attending, too. In due time his ministry spread to other cities in America and to England.

In 1871, Moody sensed his heart hungering for more of God's love and more of the Holy Spirit's power. On several occasions, two ladies sat in the front row praying while Moody preached. At the close of the service they would say to him, "We have been praying for you." "Why don't you pray for the people?" Moody would ask. "Because you need the power of the Spirit," was the reply.[21] Moody asked them to come and talk with him. They did, and poured out their hearts in prayer that he might be filled with the Holy Spirit. Moody reported, "There came a great hunger into my soul. I did not know what it was. I began to cry out as I never did before. I really felt that I did not want to live if I could not have this power for service."[22]

Shortly thereafter, Moody traveled to New York City to collect funds for people who had suffered loss during the great Chicago fire. While there he kept crying out to God to fill him with His Holy Spirit.

---

[20] Lawson, *Deeper Experiences of Famous Christians*, 242.
[21] Ibid., 246.
[22] Ibid., 246.

Well, one day, in the city of New Your – oh, what a day! – I cannot describe it, I seldom refer to it; it is almost too sacred an experience to name. ... I can only say that God revealed Himself to me, and I had such an experience of His love that I had to ask Him to stay His hand. I went to preaching again. The sermons were not different; I did not present any new truths; and yet hundreds were converted.[23]

When we are "baptized with the Holy Spirit," we, too, receive power to witness (Acts 1:8).

- We had a measure of power before.
- Following our baptism with the Holy Spirit, we receive even more. God gave Finney and Moody copious amounts. He will give to us what we need to do His bidding in our generation.

Regarding this point the Assemblies of God denomination is spot-on when it states,

Yes, when people accept Christ, the Holy Spirit ... dwells within them .... However, there is an additional and distinct ministry of the Holy Spirit called the baptism in the Holy Spirit. The Baptism is an empowering gift from God the Father that is promised to every believer (Mt. 3:11; Luke 11:13; 24:49; Acts 2:33, 38). It helps the Christian to live a holy life and also brings a new devotional attachment to Jesus Christ, making Him very real and precious. The primary purpose of the Baptism is to give greater power for witness (Acts 1:8)."[24]

All believers are entitled to receive the baptism in the Holy Spirit, and therefore should expect and earnestly

---

[23] Ibid., 247.
[24] The Assemblies of God, "Our Distinctive Doctrine: The Baptism in the Holy Spirit," page 3.

seek the promise of the Father, according to the command of our Lord Jesus Christ.[25]

Brad Long wrote,

> The baptism with the Holy Spirit is ... the conscious appropriation in faith and obedience of the empowering and equipping dimension of the Holy Spirit's work that already dwells within us. The baptism with the Holy Spirit fits within the same motif as the Spirit "upon" and has as its primary meaning empowerment for service and witness, Acts 1:5,8.[26]

E. Do We Receive More of the Holy Spirit?

When we are baptized with the Holy Spirit, in one sense we do not receive more of the Holy Spirit. The Holy Spirit is a whole Person and the whole Person of the Holy Spirit comes to live within each of us at the moment we are justified by grace through faith in Jesus Christ.

Yet, in another sense, when we are baptized with the Holy Spirit, we do receive more of the Holy Spirit.

- Before, we experienced the Holy Spirit's love, guidance, and fruit.
- After, we also experience a greater measure of His power.

---

[25] The Assemblies of God, "Our 16 Doctrines. Statement of Fundamental Truths," page 9. Phil's comment: The Assemblies of God denomination insists that speaking in tongues is *the* evidence that one has been baptized with the Holy Spirit. However, I believe it is wiser to say that speaking in tongues is one of a variety of ways the Holy Spirit affirms His empowering presence.

[26] Brad Long, Gateways, 272.

F. What happens?

Every person I know who has given serious thought to the Holy Spirit's work of empowerment struggles to put into words the answer to the question, "What happens when we are baptized with the Holy Spirit?" What spiritual transaction occurs? What happens when we experience our "personal Pentecost"?

Honestly, we do not know precisely what happens; there will always be an element of mystery. Nevertheless, I believe that the follow statements move toward describing the spiritual significance of this experience.

1. Our baptism with the Holy Spirit momentarily expands our capacity, giving the Holy Spirit more freedom to work in us and through us. We surrender, and He fills. He surges into us with greater fullness.

Contemplate this parallel: When a person has asthma, he uses an inhaler to create a capacity in his lungs to hold more air. Likewise, when we are baptized with the Holy Spirit, Jesus expands the capacity of our hearts giving the Holy Spirit more room and freedom to work in us and through us. However, we do *not* live in a state of perpetual fullness. As we engage in ministry, the Spirit who filled us flows out through us (see Mark 5:30) to bless, build up, free, heal, and restore others. In our depleted state we must return to Jesus time-and-time-again for fresh infillings, for fresh anointings, for fresh empowerment.

Cindy Stricker's Story[27]

Following her graduation from Princeton Theological Seminary, Cindy began serving as a hospital chaplain. At the

---

[27] With Cindy's permission I am including excerpts of her story from the excellent book she authored along with Brad Long and Paul Stokes, *Growing the Church in the Power of the Holy Spirit*, 31-33, 74.

same time she worked hard to obtain certification as a Clinical Pastoral Education (CPE) supervisor. "Every day," Cindy wrote, "I was busy caring for sick and dying people and their families. Several times a year I was also offering CPE classes to groups of seminary students and community clergy working under my direction at the hospital."

As if that wasn't stress enough, she dutifully carried out her role as "pastor's wife" for her husband, Steve, who served a Hungarian Reformed congregation. In addition, their young son, David, refused to sleep through the night. "I was a constant caregiver, relentlessly working to keep everything going at the hospital, with my students, and at home with my family. I knew that all this was for God, but somehow he just did not seem to be very present, and he certainly was not much help. … I was worn down, burned out, and resentful, and I knew I could not do any more. I had reached the end of my rope."

At this time, in February of 1991, Cindy's parents offered to send her and Steve to a five-day retreat titled "Gateways to Empowered Ministry," offered by Presbyterian Reformed Ministries International as part of the Dunamis Project.[28] The selling point was that her parents would keep David. Cindy wrote, "It was only when we were on the highway driving to the event that we read the brochure they had sent us and with horror realized that it was about the Holy Spirit. We nearly turned around straightaway, but the prospect of having time away from the pressures of work as well as from our sleep-resistant toddler proved too attractive. We also figured that we could skip the meetings and just enjoy being together at the beautiful conference center on the shore of Lake George in New York."

---

[28] Presbyterian Reformed Ministries International is a ministry founded in 1966 during the Charismatic renewal. The Dunamis Project is PRMI's equipping course on the Person and work of the Holy Spirit. For more information, go to www.prmi.org.

God had other plans. She found herself drawn into the teachings on the Holy Spirit and eventually asked for prayer to be baptized with the Holy Spirit. Regarding that experience, Cindy observed,

> During that Dunamis Project retreat I did not have any special experiences, such as speaking in tongues (though I have since received that particular gift of the Spirit), but when I got back to the hospital, I noticed a freshness in my work. Alongside my human labors there was now a supernatural and spiritual working of God that had not been there before. On one occasion I was ministering to a woman who had a lump on her leg, and she was terrified that it would prove to be cancer. As I was praying for her, I was surprised to have a sense that the Holy Spirit was whispering to me, "Tell her that this is not cancer." I had a tremendous struggle within myself about this. It went against all my CPE training, and I was fearful of giving her false hope born out of my spiritual enthusiasm. But the sense of guidance was persistent, and so I took what felt like a terrible risk and spoke out what I thought the Lord was saying. The change was immediate and visible, as peace came into this frightened woman. It seemed as if she was embraced by the love of Jesus, and she went into the surgery with a deep peace. Indeed, to my own surprise (and the surprise of her doctors!) the lump turned out not to be cancer.

Cindy was beginning to learn the joy and the adventure of cooperating with the Holy Spirit.

> All I knew was that the sovereign God, the Lord of the universe, had called me into a whole new dimension of working with him. I had read about it in the book of Acts but had never experienced it before in my own life and ministry. Frankly, this was a little overwhelming, but it was also immensely exciting.[29]

---

[29] *Growing the Church in the Power of the Holy Spirit*, 31-33.

Brad Long observed,

The baptism with the Holy Spirit, when understood from the biblical perspective, means to be initiated into the empowering work of the Holy Spirit. It does not have to do with coming to salvation or being sanctified. Rather, it pertains to power and equipping for witness and service. ... After the disciples received this initial experience of empowerment on Pentecost in Acts 2, we read in the rest of the book of Acts that they were filled with the Holy Spirit again and again.[30]

2. Our baptism with the Holy Spirit <u>equips us</u> to accomplish <u>special works</u> that God the Father desires to do through us.

In general, our work is to witness to Jesus and to make disciples (Acts 1:8; Matthew 28:18-20).

In particular, our callings differ.

- ✓ When the Spirit came upon Amasai, he prophesied.
- ✓ When the Spirit came upon Gideon, he rallied the troops and defeated the Midianites.
- ✓ When the Spirit came upon Saul/Paul in Acts 9, he received the grace to function as an Apostle to the Gentiles.

When we are baptized with the Holy Spirit, either Jesus activates the gifts He gave us when we initially believed in Him, and/or He down-loads (imparts) a fresh set of gifts, skills, wisdom, authority, and power, thereby equipping us to successfully fulfill our God-ordained short-term and long-term, destiny / calling / mission. A classic illustration of this is Bezalel. The Spirit filled him thereby equipping him to

---

[30] Brad Long, *Moving With The Spirit*, April 2012, Volume 212, page 2. Dr. Long expressed a similar thought in *Gateways to Empowered Ministry: The Person and Work of the Holy Spirit* (PRMI, revised 1997), 251.

accomplish his calling, namely, to oversee the construction of the Tabernacle (Exodus 35:30-35).

Likewise, when the Holy Spirit comes upon us, He down-loads the skill-set we need to accomplish a special work.

- ✓ Speak a prophetic word
- ✓ Serve as a conduit for Jesus' healing power
- ✓ Interpret a message given in tongues
- ✓ Help parents parent
- ✓ Restore marriages
- ✓ Shepherd a flock
- ✓ Build an orphanage
- ✓ Paint a picture
- ✓ Rescue women from the sex trade
- ✓ Intercede
- ✓ Launch a training and equipping center
- ✓ Discern the spirit that is behind a person's words and actions

Susan Finck's Story
revsf6@sbcglobal.net

Here's a little bit of my [Susan's] journey into the empowering work of the Holy Spirit.

> 1) In college, I attended a Dallas-seminary Bible church[31] that was both loving and counter cultural. I tell my kids it was a 'hippie church.' Home group every Thursday. Prayer was always one way (we talk to God). Lots of emphasis on learning. I was moving towards marriage with a very godly guy who adored me. Yet "something" was preventing me from becoming engaged. Looking back, it was the Holy Spirit. I was searching and the church's leaders gave me a book

---

[31] Dallas Seminary is an excellent Bible-believing, Bible-teaching seminary that is cessationist. It believes that manifestational gifts such as healing, tongues, and prophecy ceased as soon as the last book of the New Testament had been written.

called *Decision Making and the Will of God* which stated basically that if the choice we are considering doesn't violate Scripture, we can do what we want. They counseled me to "not follow my feelings" and marry him because he was a wise choice, saying that God didn't speak specifically, etc. This didn't ring true and put me on a search.

2) As a young single, I joined First Pres/SA. I was curious about tongues, so I asked my pastor. He offered to "get a team and lay hands on me and ask for that gift." I didn't want it that bad! I was fearful but I continued to thirst.

3) A couple of years later, I was a seminary student at a liberal PCUSA seminary. My husband was in an evangelical pastors' prayer group, and some of the wives attended a night time "bible study" hosted by some Pentecostal ladies. Blew my mind! This was not really a "bible study" at all. One of the gals would "get" these first-person messages (she called them prophecies) for individuals or for the group. Most of them had the ring of truth for me, though I didn't understand it. People got healed on the spot. I saw my first deliverance (complete with screaming and writhing.) As soon as the girl started to manifest, I said I needed to leave. The older woman who co-hosted said, "Do not leave; you are needed." I was flooded with an authoritative supernatural calm, and all during the deliverance I somehow "knew" where they should go next as they ministered to her. I could see the demons were hiding and what was really going on. I had no idea how I knew but I did. They told me I was "flowing in words of knowledge." I must say that I always had an academic belief that demons were real and that God "could" move in supernatural ways. For some reason I had bought into the notion that it was usually in Africa or some primitive area.

At this group, all prayer was two-way. God always spoke, and often in King James English. :) The group attracted me, freaked me out, and made me question ... all in one. They argued about whether I was "saved and filled" or just "saved." They believed that everyone who was "filled" had a prayer language. But they were very loving and God was real and on the move!

4) During this season, I noticed in a PCC newsletter that they had hired a new director who was available to come speak. In my role as chair of our Presbytery's Church Growth and Renewal committee, I invited Brad Long to speak at a Presbytery conference. He was "fresh off the boat." :) He invited me to Dunamis in Lake George where I really appreciated the theological foundation/grid and the discernment/debriefing process. I encountered other people who were well educated and more my "tribe" who were also moving with the Holy Spirit.

G. Initial Evidence of Empowerment

When a person is initially baptized with the Holy Spirit, often he or she will experience some evidence of the Holy Spirit's empowering presence. Each person's experience will be different. Some people, but not all, will speak in tongues (Acts 2:1-4; 10:44-48; 19:1-7). In addition, newly Spirit-baptized individuals may experience:

- ✓ A hunger for the Word
- ✓ Spontaneous praise, thanksgiving, and worship
- ✓ Shaking and trembling
- ✓ Heat
- ✓ Laughter
- ✓ Deep peace
- ✓ Resting in the Spirit
- ✓ … or nothing at all

When Brad Long prayed for his pastor to be baptized with the Holy Spirit, Richard felt disappointed because he had no sense that God was doing anything special in his life. Richard states, "I felt like a rock." The next Sunday, however, Brad's daughter, who also attended Richard's church, called home all excited. "Daddy, Daddy! It was like Richard stopped speaking and God started talking through him!" To this day the anointing of the Holy Spirit rests upon Richard almost every time he stands to preach.

In *Growing the Church in the Power of the Holy Spirit*, Cindy Stricker reflected on her journey and wrote,

> During that week [at Lake George] I did experience Jesus' love and healing, which were wonderful, but when a few people laid hands on me and prayed for me to be baptized with the Holy Spirit, it seemed that nothing at all happened. I just asked and, in … "naked faith," I accepted the empowerment of the Holy Spirit that I needed. There were no emotions, no tongues, no fireworks at all – just a deep peace. It was only later when I got back to work in the hospital that I discovered that the Holy Spirit had given spiritual gifts to lead me in knowing how to pray for patients. As I stepped out in obedience, I saw the power of God at work through me.
>
> That took place seventeen years ago, and since then I have experienced some times of great struggle in my life, such as when my husband, Steve was diagnosed with brain cancer. But as I have walked in obedience, God has filled me with the Holy Spirit again and again, empowering me for teaching and for healing ministry, and also for growing the Dunamis Fellowship. It truly has been a wonderful journey that just keeps getting more and more exciting.[32]

---

[32] *Growing the Church in the Power of the Holy Spirit*, 74.

Dr. Reuben Archer Torrey's Story

R.A. Torrey's (1856-1928) credentials are remarkable. He was a rich man's son, a college graduate, and an intellectual who, after studying theology at Yale, Leipzig and Erlangen, read the New Testament in Greek each day and the Old Testament in Hebrew. D. L. Moody chose Torrey to serve as the superintendent of the Bible Institute in Chicago, known today as Moody Bible Institute. If this scholar and educator needed to be baptized with the Holy Spirit, how much more do we!

I had been a minister for some years before I came to the place where I saw that I had no right to preach until I was definitely baptized with the Holy Ghost. I went to a business friend of mine and said to him in private, "I am never going to enter my pulpit again until I have been baptized with the Holy Spirit and know it, or until God in some way tells me to go." Then, just as far as I could, I shut myself up alone in my study and spent the time continually on my knees asking God to baptize me with the Holy Spirit. As the days passed, the devil tried to tempt me by saying, "Suppose Sunday comes and you are not baptized with the Holy Spirit, what then?" I replied, "Whatever comes, I will not go into my pulpit and preach again until I have been baptized with the Holy Spirit and know it, or God in some way tells me to go; even though I have to tell my people that I have never been fit to preach." But Sunday did not come before the blessing came. I had it more or less definitely mapped out in my mind what would happen; but what I had mapped out in my mind did not happen. I recall the exact spot where I was kneeling in prayer in my study. I could go to the very spot in that house at 1348 N. Adams Street in Minneapolis. It was a very quiet moment, one of the most quiet moments I ever knew; indeed, I think one reason I had to wait so long was because it took that long before my soul could get quiet before God. Then God simply said to me, not in any audible voice, but in my heart, "It's yours. Now go and preach."[33]

Sometime after this experience (I do not recall just how long after), while sitting in my room one day, that very same room, I recall just where I was sitting, before my revolving bookcase, I do not know whether I was thinking about this subject at all, I do not remember, but suddenly as near as I can describe it, though it does not exactly describe it, I was struck from my chair on to the floor and I found myself shouting (I was not brought up to shout and I am not of a shouting temperament, but I shouted like the loudest shouting Methodist) "glory to God, glory to God, glory to God," and I could not stop. I tried to stop, but it was just as if some other power than my own was moving my jaws. At last, when I had succeeded in pulling myself together, I went downstairs and told my wife what had happened.

But that was not when I was baptized with the Holy Spirit. I was baptized with the Holy Spirit when I took Him by simple faith in the naked Word of God, and anyone of you can be thus baptized today, yes, you can be thus baptized before you leave this building this afternoon.[34]

H. When are we Baptized with the Holy Spirit?

One of the debates in Christian circles pertains to the question of "when." When are we baptized with the Holy Spirit?

---

[33] Dr. Reuben Archer Torrey, *The Holy Spirit: Who He Is and What He Does* (Classic Books for Today, NO. 152, 2000), 54-55.

[34] Ibid., 55.

Based on his understanding of 1 Corinthians 12:12, esteemed pastor and theologian John Stott insists that our baptism with the Holy Spirit always occurs at the time of our conversion.

Sometimes that is exactly what happens. However, Biblical models demonstrate that for some, a season of time elapses between their conversion and their baptism with the Holy Spirit.

A. Biblical evidence for a <u>one-step process</u>: Conversion and empowerment occurring on the same occasion.

Saul, Acts 9

> *So Ananias departed and entered the house. And laying his hands on him he said, "Brother Saul, the Lord Jesus who appeared to you on the road by which you came has sent me so that you may regain your sight and be <u>filled</u>[35] with the Holy Spirit." 18 And immediately something like scales fell from his eyes, and he regained his sight. Then he rose and was <u>baptized</u>;[36] and taking food, he was strengthened. Acts 9:17-19, ESV*

Cornelius' Household, Acts 10

> *<u>While Peter was still speaking</u> these words, <u>the Holy Spirit came on all</u> who heard the message. [45]The circumcised believers who had come with Peter were astonished that the gift of the Holy Spirit had been poured out even on the Gentiles. [46]For they heard them speaking in tongues and praising God. [47]Then Peter said, "Can anyone keep these people from being <u>baptized with water</u>? They have received the Holy Spirit just as we have." [48]So he ordered that they be baptized in the name of Jesus Christ. Then they asked Peter to stay with them for a few days.*

---

[35] Here, meaning "empowered." See our chapter, "The Dual Meaning of 'Filled.'"

[36] Water baptism, here signifying conversion.

B. Biblical evidence for a <u>two-step process</u>: First the grace of conversion, and later, the grace of empowerment.

A. Converted	B. Empowered
And with that he[Jesus] breathed on them [His disciples] and said, "Receive the Holy Spirit. John 20:22 … and that is exactly what happened: the disciples received the Holy Spirit. They opened the door and welcomed Him in. The Holy Spirit came to dwell within them. "The Holy Spirit came to live in them, bringing their spirits to life – they were born again of the Spirit."[37]	Fifty days after they received the Holy Spirit, they were baptized with the Holy Spirit on the Day of Pentecost (Acts 2:1-4).

Personally, I (Phil) experienced a two-step process. When I was eleven years old, I was born again. Thirty-nine years later, following a series of teaching on the Person and work of the Holy Spirit, a few people gathered around me and together we invited Jesus to baptize me with the Holy Spirit. On that occasion I felt almost nothing at all. However, a few weeks later I became aware of spontaneous praise and worship bubbling up within me. I could not stop worshipping. Even with that, I was not sure that God had answered our prayers. As I walked alone in the woods behind our home in Traverse City, MI, I kept crying out, "Jesus, baptize me with Your Holy

---

[37] Dennis and Rita Bennett, *The Holy Spirit and You* (Kingsway Publications, 1974), 26.

Spirit!" A few days later while praying that same prayer, I "heard" the Holy Spirit's distinct response, "I already have."

Our initial baptism with the Holy Spirit is our personal Pentecost. From that time forward, during *kairos* moments the Holy Spirit comes "upon" us in power and enables us to speak anointed words and/or do mighty works in order to advance the Father's agenda for a person and/or situation. From that point on, the Holy Spirit who is already in us, flows out through us in powerful ways (words and/or works) on an as-needed basis to impact others for good.

I. How to Receive the Baptism with the Holy Spirit

The short answer is:

- Examine your heart in light of Scripture and affirm that you are a Christian.
- Confess all known sins and turn from them.
- Look to Jesus and, in faith, ask Him to baptize you with the Holy Spirit.
    - o It is often helpful to have trusted friends, especially those who are in positions of spiritual authority and have an understanding of Spirit-baptism, to lay hands on you and join with you in this prayer.
- Wait quietly in Jesus' presence. Respond in obedience to His nudges or prompts, if any.
- Believe in faith that Jesus has heard your prayer and will answer it in His time and in His way.
- Continue to abide in Christ and in His Word.

At the end of my post in PastorsPub.net entitled *"Joel 2:28-32 and Pentecost: Surprisingly Good News,"* you will find a link to two brief videos that speak in a compelling manner about how to receive the baptism with the Holy Spirit.

Joanne Rozendaal's Story

Joanne lives in Edmonton, Alberta, Canada. She participates on the prayer ministry team in her church and serves on the leadership team for Dunamis, Canada. She and her husband, Curt, love to cycle. Here is her story.

I [Joanne] grew up in a home where we were always going to church. Eventually, as an adult in my 30's, something began to stir in me and I thought, "There must be more to the Christian life than I am experiencing." Reading the Book of Acts only intensified my thirst and frustration because I did not see any action like that in my life or circle of friends.

One Sunday I read an announcement in our bulletin that Brad Long would be teaching at a nearby church on the Holy Spirit. Immediately I wanted to attend because I was seeking greater understanding about the role of the Holy Spirit in our lives today. I went excited and fearful, and my husband, Curt, went with me. Before the evening was over, Curt had a vision, which was a really new experience for him! Even though nothing at all happened in my life, I continued to have an inner drive to learn more. We became a conference junkies and went to every group I could find that talked about the Holy Spirit. In time my daughter-in-law invited me to attend a Woman's Aglow conference near my home in Edmonton, Alberta, Canada. A compelling speaker shared a dream she had about a big library. In the dream God put His finger on one line in one book and said, "This is all you know about Me." "You're right!" I said to myself. "God is so big! and I know so little about Him."

In my church, prayer was not evident other than during the service, but at this Woman's Aglow meeting, everyone around me respond to the invitation for prayer. So I got in line. As my line inched forward I thought to myself, "What will I ask for? I'm not even sure why I'm in line." When I stood before the prayer ministry team, they asked how they could pray for me. To my surprise I heard myself say, "Surrender." As soon as they began to pray for me, something shifted deep within me and I received the gift of tongues. I certainly was not seeking that gift, and since I was from a Christian Reformed Church background, this was a shock! They continued to pray for me and next thing I knew I was resting in the Spirit on the floor. Unbelievable! The ladies wisely counseled me to just rest for a little while longer and let the Holy Spirit work in me. They hovered near and kept praying, and I really appreciated that.

Before I drove home that evening I called Curt and told him, "You'll never believe what happened to me! They prayed for me and I received the gift of tongues!" His response really surprised me and warmed my heart. "I've been praying for you all day that you would."

Providentially, the ladies who prayed for me had warned me that the enemy would mess with my mind. Sure enough, he did. As I drove home questions came such as, "Did I just make that up? Did that really happen?" Within moments the Holy Spirit assured me, "No that was really real."

The next morning we went to our home church and my heart experienced times of refreshing. Tears filled my eyes as we sang the same old hymns that I had sung for years. To my surprise I heard myself singing in tongues! Curt heard me too and smiled knowingly. At the end of the service I told a trusted wise man in our congregation who was Spirit filled, what was happening. He was overjoyed. However, I did not say much of anything to anyone else for about three years. I wanted to learn more before making my new-found relationship with the Holy Spirit public.

Eventually the Lord led me to attend a series of Dunamis Conferences sponsored by Presbyterian Reformed Ministries International, the organization where Brad Long was the Executive Director. Very helpful! In time I invited others from our church who I sensed were thirsting for more of Jesus to join me. One lady resisted somewhat saying, "I will come with you as long as there's no fu-fu." Although I was not sure what she meant by "fu-fu," I responded, "Just come." She did, and so did 8-10 others. My friend is now a Spirit-filled point person for the prayer ministry in our church. Today the prayer culture of our church is changing for good, praise God!

J. An Analogy: A Benefit of Baptism with the Holy Spirit

Logos[38] is the name of a company that markets eBooks to church leaders. For the sake of illustration, let's use round numbers. Let's say that the company's entry-level package includes access to 100 of the 500 books in their library. As soon as we purchase their software, we have access to 100 books and the quality of these books is excellent. We have sufficient study materials to last a lifetime.

Logos also sells upgrades. For an additional fee they will unlock three hundred more books, making them available to us.

Spiritual Parallel

1. As soon as we become Christians, the whole Holy Spirit comes to live within us and He begins to teach us, guide us, and transform us from the inside out. Jesus makes some of the functional gifts of the Holy Spirit (Romans 12:1-8) available to us.

2. When we are baptized with the Holy Spirit, we do not receive more of the Holy Spirit. Rather, Jesus unlocks a greater measure of access:

    A. To me by the Holy Spirit.
    B. To the Holy Spirit by me.

---

[38] https://www.logos.com

Specifically, we tap into the power dimension of the Holy Spirit and Jesus unlocks the <u>manifestational gifts</u> of the Spirit (1 Corinthians 12:7-11).[39]

Why do we need more power?

- ❖ In order to serve in our world with even greater effectiveness as Jesus' witnesses.
- ❖ In order to fulfill our destinies.

Please understand that following our "baptism with the Holy Spirit," i.e., our "personal Pentecost," we do *not* live in a permanent state of empowerment. Rather, we only experience increased power whenever the Holy Spirit comes "upon us,"[40] or "clothes us.[41]" We refer to this as the "episodic" nature of empowerment.

When Jesus' agenda for us in a particular situation has been accomplished, the Spirit "lifts" and His power diminishes until our next assignment.

Empowerment is Episodic

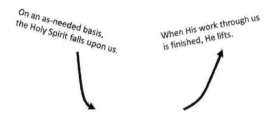

On an as-needed basis, the Holy Spirit falls upon us.

When His work through us is finished, He lifts.

---

[39] For a helpful understanding of spiritual gifts and a concise definition of each, go to "<u>Spiritual Gifts: Tools for Building</u>," https://docs.google.com/document/d/19x5NA9Qy_CYkCoYEYJ25VUVlN c0TRh20QxoFSawsaYw/edit#heading=h.gjdgxs

[40] Acts 1:8

[41] "... clothed with power from on high." Luke 24:49, ESV

Illustration: The Holy Spirit "Lifted" for a Season

Following a brief sabbatical, Jay Knoblock felt refreshed and stepped back into ministry in January 2018. Jay wrote,

> University and conference teaching, board meetings, and a re-commissioning service for my expanding ministry in Asia were all a part of a busy and productive January. Through it all, I watched the Lord move powerfully through me and I felt blessed.
>
> Yet when January ended I found myself in an odd place. My formal teaching was over. While I was open for evangelistic opportunities, it was winter time and not as easy to do outreach. Many of my local disciples were growing up and needed less mentoring. As I prayed about the equipping group that I had been co-leading on Thursday nights prior to my sabbatical, I was shown to help coach leaders but not to lead or teach. Everything seemed to be fading. It was a little disorienting.
>
> Time can go by so quickly when the Spirit is using and empowering us. Yet we must remember that the Spirit empowers us to complete the tasks *He* desires us to accomplish. While the Spirit constantly indwells us, we are not constantly experiencing the "power" of God in the same way. In late January of 2018, I was experiencing something I had experienced before and probably will again: the Spirit had "lifted." It was time for a different season.
>
> This was especially odd to me fresh off of a sabbatical. It was tempting to try to "make things happen" and say, "Yes" to things I wasn't called to do in order to get the thrill of more "outward" ministry. Yet God warned me against doing so. I remember writing my intercessory prayer team and asking for prayers that I would be "productive" in the weeks before going to Asia in mid-

March. Yet what did productivity even look like?
Thankfully, after a short time of bewilderment, God
showed me!

God guided me into a time of rich intimacy with Him
including an expanded time of prayer and Scripture
reading. He also answered a past prayer request – a
request to learn the Korean (and Japanese) languages at
a greater level. I had a grace to study the language for
several hours a day! Thank you Jesus! February and
early March of 2018 were some of the most productive
times I have ever had both in God's Word and in
language learning to date. And, as I was obedient in
these areas, there were still some moments when I
experienced the empowerment of the Spirit for short
bits of informal teaching, prophecy, discipleship, etc.
However, it was just not the primary focus for that
season.

God desires us be obedient to His leading and peace
comes when we do so. I have very fond memories of
January, February, and early March of 2018. While the
outward empowering of the Holy Spirit was more
evident in January, God was likewise with me in other
enriching ways in February and March. Praise the
Lord!

JayKnoblock125@gmail.com

K. Synonyms

Different words, essentially the same meaning:

Baptized with the Holy Spirit	Mt.3:11-12; Mark 1:6-8; Luke 3:16-17; John 1:32-34; Acts 1:4-5; Luke 24:49; Acts 11:16
Filled with the Holy Spirit	Luke 1:41-42, 67-68; Acts 2:4, 4:7-8, 31; Acts 9:17, 13:8-9
Spirit on or upon	Luke 2:25, 4:18; Acts 1:8, 19:5-6
Holy Spirit fell on	Acts 8:16; Acts 11:15
Clothed with power	Luke 24:49; Judges 6:34
Spirit poured out	Acts 2:33, 10:45
Receive the Holy Spirit	Acts 8:14-17, 10:47
Anointed / Fresh Anointing	Luke 4:18; Acts 10:38; 1 John 2:20

We do not control how much power we will receive, how often we will receive it, or the purpose for which it will be given. Rather, we are instruments through whom Jesus plays His music. Our role is to trust and obey. When we do so, we join the energizing "dance of cooperation" with the Father, Son, and Holy Spirit.

To use another analogy, water flows steadily through a one-inch pipe. When the size of the pipe increases at its source from one inch to three inches, more water flows in the same amount of time. When the Holy Spirit's work through us for a particular occasion is finished and He "lifts," the pipe returns to its normal size.

It is wisest to follow Scripture's example and use "baptism with the Holy Spirit" to describe our <u>initial</u> experience of empowerment and use terms such as "filled with the Holy Spirit," and "anointed" to describe <u>subsequent</u> experiences of empowerment.

Remember Gideon's encounter with the angel?

> *Then the angel of the Lord reached out the tip of the staff that was in his hand and <u>touched</u> the meat and the unleavened cakes. And <u>fire sprang up</u> from the rock and consumed the meat and the unleavened cakes.* Judges 6:21, ESV

On divinely ordained occasions subsequent to our initial experience of empowerment,

- when the Father has something He wants done in another person's life,
- and when He sovereignly chooses to use us as an instrument through whom He will work,
- and when our hearts and hands are willing to cooperate with Him,

at these *kairos* moments we experience a special touch, a special anointing and, figuratively "fire springs up." The Holy Spirit springs into action. As we cooperate with Him, the Father works through us by the power of the Holy Spirit to advance His agenda for that particular person, time, and place. Once the Holy Spirit has accomplished the Father's objective, He "lifts."

Illustration: Learning the Joy of Cooperating with the Holy Spirit's Gentle Nudge
By Tamera Brockman

> I was in a class where we were encouraged to step out in new, creative ways to work with the Holy Spirit in

worship. A couple of canvases and paint supplies were available for anyone who wanted to try to "paint with the Holy Spirit" as we were singing and praising God.

I had some interest but felt a bit shy or intimidated about going and painting on one of the easels. I think the Holy Spirit gave me a nudge of encouragement to go paint at the easel. It was just that - a spiritual nudge, not physical, just mental or spiritual or both. I let fear get in the way and argued with the nudge. I resisted by telling the Holy Spirit that I would not know what to paint. The Holy Spirit actually countered my argument with an idea! The idea came to me that I could paint a picture of some of the American Sign Language Signs I was using in worship. One sign was for "sing" and one was for "faithful." It was a rather unusual idea for a painting subject. I must have also been given confidence or motivation from the Holy Spirit because after that I obeyed. I went and painted those signs and more. Obedience brings joy!

L. Frequency of Empowerment

Following our initial baptism with the Holy Spirit, how often does the average Christian experience a special anointing by the Holy Spirit for a particular work?

That is a good question. Some of my coworkers seem to dream dreams, see visions, speak prophetically, impart healing, and receive words of knowledge on a daily basis. When I am around them, I can feel second rate. Other coworkers may experience the Holy Spirit "falling upon them" once or twice per year. My personal experience is that I cannot predict when the Spirit's anointing will come nor can I control how often it occurs. Sometimes Holy fire falls; on many other occasions, the functional gifts (see Romans 12) undergird my ministry. Hopefully, on all occasions the fruit of the Spirit seasons my service.

Experiences of empowerment can become addicting. We may find ourselves longing for another spiritual "high." When it does not happen for a season, we may begin to doubt. The following entry from my journal points to this reality.

December 27, 2014. San Diego, CA

> *Thus the Lord said to me: "Go, set a*
> *watchman; let him announce what he sees."*
> *Isaiah 21:6, ESV*

After reading Isaiah's words about the watchman's role, I attended a prayer session in preparation for the Chinese Mission Convention. During the opening song I had a strong sense that someone in the group – perhaps the whole group – was very dry and depleted spiritually. Preparation for the mission convention combined with the demands of the Christmas season took a lot out of us. I prayed, "Lord, what am I supposed to do with this awareness?" I waited and wondered, and the meeting continued. A couple times I glanced over my shoulder at the group, and the eyes of my heart focused on a lady whom I will call Lilly.

At a transition point, John, who was leading the session, asked me to offer a prayer. "Thank you, Jesus," I said in my heart. "This is Your time." I stepped to the front of the group and said, "I have a strong sense that we as a group are to gather around Lilly and pray for her." I turned to John and asked, "Is that ok?" He nodded "Yes," and I invited Lilly to come to the front and sit in a chair. After a little encouragement due to the newness of this process for some, the rest of the group gathered around her.

"Lilly, may we lay hands on you as we pray?" I asked.

"Yes."

As soon as I placed my hand on her head, I sensed the Holy Spirit come upon me and my hand and arm began to tremble. Quietly and with compassion the Holy Spirit prompted me to pray, "Lord Jesus, refresh her. Lord Jesus, fill her with living water. Lord Jesus, minister renewal to Lilly."

Others joined me in offering prayers for her. An intense sense of the Lord's presence lasted for about ten minutes.

After sensing that the Spirit had lifted, I concluded the prayer time by sealing the work that God had done. "We seal the work that Jesus is doing in your life, Lilly, in the Name of the Father, Son, and Holy Spirit." She gave me a hug and I sat down with a heart overflowing with gratitude. Why gratitude? Because it had been a long while since I felt such clear guidance from the Lord for a ministry situation. Honestly, I wondered if the Lord had put me on the shelf now that *FireStarter* had been published. This experience reassured me of Jesus' commitment to continue using me in spiritually significant ways in people's lives. All glory to Him!

5. In Essentials, Unity

For older generations, labels such as "Pentecostal" and "Spirit-filled" often led to raw debates and real divisions within churches. However, younger generations are far removed from long-standing disagreements about "the validity of spiritual gifts, the role of expressive forms of worship, and about the need for receiving personal direction from the Holy Spirit."[42] For many of them, it is all good. Subsequently, younger generations spend very little time defending their views, which in turn, may leave them wondering what they really do believe about the Person and work of the Holy Spirit in our lives in our day, and why it matters.

Adam's Story

Adam serves as an intern for Presbyterian Reformed Ministries International in Black Mountain, NC. Typical of many people his age (29), Adam has sampled a variety theological streams including Christian Missionary Alliance (CMA), Reformed Dispensational, an "Acts 29 Church" that emphasized social justice, and a Presbyterian Church that welcomed all the gifts and manifestations of the Holy Spirit. "I've tried a lot," said Adam.

Adam describes himself as an abstract thinker who loves stories and includes parable-like narratives whenever he has an opportunity to teach. When I [Phil] asked him if he could point to a defining moment when he was baptized with the Holy Spirit, his response was slow and thoughtful. "No. It seems like I just grew into understanding and practicing being guided by the Holy Spirit." When I asked him for an example, he responded quickly by telling me a story. "Normally, I am very guarded when I am around Sally (not her real name) because we usually have conflicts. However, on one occasion she was telling me about her view of a person to whom she was ministering, and something struck me. I responded with uncharacteristic quickness and with an authority in my voice that was not my own, 'That's wrong! What you are saying is not true!'" Another person who was part of the conversation quickly confirmed this perspective.

---

[42] David Kinnaman, president of the Barna Group. "How Different Generations View and Engage with Charismatic and Pentecostal Christianity." https://www.barna.org. March 29, 2010

Adam summarized by saying, "My theology of Holy Spirit was good before I came to PRMI but while I'm here I am seeing ways I want it to grow. For example, I had not made a distinction between the Holy Spirit's work *in* us transforming our character, and the Holy Spirit coming *upon* us to empower us for ministry. My theology is developing," he said, "and so are my experiences of the empowering work of the Holy Spirit."

Adam Rampersaud
adam@prmi.org

A. Charismatic

Do not let the term scare you: in a sense, every Christian is charismatic.

> *Having gifts (charisma) that differ according to the grace (charis) given to us, let us use them ... Romans 12:6, ESV*

> *As each has received a gift (charisma), use it to serve one another, as good stewards of God's varied grace (charis). 1 Peter 4:10, ESV*

Based on the above verses John Stott astutely observed,

> The whole church is a Charismatic community. Every member has a [spiritual] gift (*charismata*); hence, every member is Charismatic.[43]

The point is this: From a Biblical perspective every Christian is, in fact, charismatic. However, popular usage of the term still leads, on occasion, to real divisions within the Body of Christ. From the perspective of the average person, some Christians

---

[43] John Stott, *God's New Society: The Message of Ephesians*, 156.

are charismatic and others are not. "Charismatics," as the average person sees it, lift their hands in worship, speak in tongues, love repetitious worship choruses, and engage in TV showmanship.

"I don't want to be one of them," they say. "They are much to emotional and mindless for my tastes."

In reality, John Stott is right. Even though we may hold different views on issues such as the baptism with the Holy Spirit, and even though we may express our faith differently, every Christian is charismatic. Let us strive to put into practice the creed penned by Rupertus Meldenius, a German Lutheran theologian of the early seventeenth century:[44]

> In Essentials Unity,
> In Non-Essentials Liberty,
> In All Things Charity.

B. Modern Charismatics

The majority of charismatic people and churches hold classic Evangelical beliefs such as the five *solas* of the Reformation:

1. *Sola Scriptura* ("Scripture alone"): The Bible alone is our highest authority.
2. *Sola Fide* ("faith alone"): We are saved through faith alone in Jesus Christ.
3. *Sola Gratia* ("grace alone"): We are saved by the grace of God alone, not by our works.
4. *Solus Christus* ("Christ alone"): Jesus Christ alone is our Lord, Savior, and King.
5. *Soli Deo Gloria* ("to the glory of God alone"): We live for the glory of God alone.

---

[44] *In Essentials Unity, In Non-Essentials Liberty, In All Things Charity* by Mark Ross. Tabletalk Magazine. https://www.ligonier.org/learn/articles/essentials-unity-non-essentials-liberty-all-things/

Evangelicals who are charismatic in the popular sense of the term add to the above an emphasis on the Person and work of the Holy Spirit, especially, the empowering work of the Holy Spirit.[45]

Pamela Starr Dewey assessed the situation well when she wrote,

> The word "Charismatic" has come to be an adjective attached to those individuals and groups who *disagree* with the conclusion that the supernatural gifts of the spirit are no longer manifested in the world. Charismatics believe that all of the gifts are still available to the Christian community. In fact, the term Charismatic usually implies in particular those "supernatural" gifts—sometimes called "sign gifts," as they are viewed as an outward "sign" of the power of the Holy Spirit—such as "speaking in tongues" and "prophecy" and "discernment of spirits."[46]

Every Christian group has its "spin" on Scripture. Baptists have their spin; so do Presbyterians, Methodists, Congregationalists, and Pentecostals. We all read the same words in the same Bible but our interpretations differ, and hence, our practices diverge.[47]

---

[45] My book, *FireStarter: The Holy Spirit Empowers,* chronicles my theological and experiential journey from being a die-hard dispensational cessationist to embracing and practicing Charismatic Christianity.

[46] Pamela Starr Dewey, Pentecostal and Charismatic– What's the Difference?   http://www.isitso.org/guide/pentchar.html

[47] I am not implying that it does not matter how we interpret Scripture because it does matter. See my book on hermeneutics entitled *Gleaning Meaning From God's Word: Better Bible Study Helps.*

Charismatic Christians and Charismatic churches are usually characterized by:

1. A spiritual hunger for God and His Word.

Recently, a young charismatic traveled to stay in our home for a brief vacation. On the first day of his vacation, he spent 3-4 hours studying Scripture. When I returned from the office that evening, he joyfully described his refreshing, enriching time in the Word.

Not long ago, I listened attentively as man in his early 20s described an encounter with Jesus Christ that transformed his dark world – a double life that included pornography, violent video games, and schemes to hurt others. "The people in that Bible study prayed for me," he said, "and the Holy Spirit felt hot in my heart. It was amazing! In all my years of being a 'Sunday Christian' I've never experienced anything like that." He continued by saying, "I had this hunger to read the Bible. I read the entire New Testament in one weekend."

James Kearny's Story

Currently James lives in Seattle, WA, and serves under the umbrella of Presbyterian Reformed Ministries International (PRMI) as the "Developer of Congregational Dunamis." jdkearny@gmail.com

James was raised Catholic and met the Lord as a result of a vision he received on the night of his confirmation. "I had a genuine relationship with God through Jesus Christ," said James. During his college days at Yale University he partied through the week, getting high and listening to music. He was very popular and had a string of girlfriends. On Sundays he went to church. When he paused long enough to think about life, he had to admit that he felt a deep discontentment.

"After graduation, I [James] went on a round the world tour with a dozen guys in a singing group, the Whiffenpoofs. In the first leg of the tour, my best friend, Rob, got saved. That was a big deal! Rob had gone to a Bible study led by a group of moms he knew. Rob reported, 'After one of our meetings, they put a chair in the center of the room and I sat in it. They laid hands on me and prayed, and I was baptized with the Holy Spirit. Then, we all had ice cream.'"

"That sounds cool!" said James. "Do you think they would pray for me?"

"Sure."

James went to the study and sat in the chair in the center of the circle. The moms laid hands on him and invited Jesus to baptize him with the Holy Spirit. Then, they all had ice cream. Nothing emotional happened. But later he felt a huge sense of relief. As James tells it, "We went around the world studying the Bible and growing in our faith. For example, I got the gift of tongues on a plane between LA and Japan."

I [Phil] laughed and asked, "How did that happen?"

"A guy in the group said, 'Here's how to speak in tongues.' I said, 'Ok,' and did it."

"Was it real?" I asked.

"I've been praying in tongues every day ever since."

James reported that when he came back from the world tour, his life was changed in part because he had devoted hours to reading his Bible. He had intended to head to NYC to become an actor. Before going he set aside a day for prayer and fasting in order to hear from God about going to NYC.

James began the day by praying, "Lord, I want to go to New York." Then he paused and said, "Lord, what do You think?"

He sensed that God had a Scripture for him. So he played "Bible roulette." He closed his eyes, opened his Bible, and his finger landed on Isaiah 30.

> *"Ah, stubborn children," declares the Lord,*
> *"who carry out a plan, but not mine,*
> *and who make an alliance, but not of my Spirit,*
> *   that they may add sin to sin;*
> *who set out to go down to Egypt,*
> *   without asking for my direction,*
> *to take refuge in the protection of Pharaoh*
> *   and to seek shelter in the shadow of Egypt!*
> *Therefore shall the protection of Pharaoh turn to your shame,*
> *   and the shelter in the shadow of Egypt to your humiliation. Isaiah 30:1-3, ESV*

"Ok, Lord, I won't go to New York."

Next, he asked God, "So what do I do now?" He looked down at his Bible again and a Scripture lit up. *"You will hear a voice behind you saying this is the way, walk in it, whether you turn to the right or turn to the left." Isaiah 30:21*

In light of these verses, James decided to become a hard-core follower of Jesus Christ. He attended a megachurch in Atlanta, spent 8 hours a day reading the Bible, and became a super Christian. He worked as a carpenter rebuilding houses for $2 an hour and lived with his parents. Later he moved out and shared an apartment with some friends from church. God provided. He still works from time to time as a carpenter.

James could not maintain the intensity of his spiritual life in Atlanta. Eventually he crashed and burned. A few years later, by God's grace, he was introduced to balanced teaching about the Person and work of the Holy Spirit through the Dunamis Project sponsored by Presbyterian Reformed Ministries International. "Through Dunamis I learned a sane, sustainable theology for developing a relationship with the Father, Son, and Holy Spirit. I'm still practicing things today that I learned from them. In fact, I am working with teams of anointed leaders to help people discover the joy of this journey of staying in step with the Spirit."

"What would you say to someone who feels a tinge of discontent with life and senses a stirring in their heart?" I asked.

Following a thoughtful moment James responded, "God is reaching out to you. He is beginning to call you to a deeper engagement with Himself. Seek Him. Read the Bible. Talk to Christians whom you respect who have a growing relationship with the Holy Spirit. You will find many of them in Dunamis."

2. A desire to welcome the manifestations of the Holy Spirit for the common good.[48]

During small group meetings, mid-sized gatherings, and larger worship services, charismatics create space for the Holy Spirit to move and to manifest His presence among them. Teaching, prophecy, tongues, interpretation, lifting hands, spontaneous and exuberant worship, verbal praise such as "Hallelujah", "glory to God", "praise You Jesus", "I love you Lord", "thank you Lord", and singing in the Spirit are experienced as "normal" in charismatic gatherings. The agenda of the church's leaders is secondary; Jesus' agenda through Scripture and through the Holy Spirit is primary.

Illustration: God's Grand Finale
By Jay Knoblock
www.spiritualstrengthtraining.com
July 2018

The end of July found me [Jay] in rural Black Mountain, NC, teaching at a youth leadership camp called Upward

---

[48] See 1 Corinthians 12:7-11

Challenge. I always enjoy these camps as they utilize the teaching we have from the Dunamis Institute in a way appropriate for youth. In addition to our regular teaching times, there were small groups, service projects, an outreach time, and times for leisure and games.

One other daily time on our schedule was the evening sessions. These were times where we never really knew what God was going to do. Rather, we would discern together as a leadership team who would be on point for leadership and prayerfully discern a general idea of what God wanted to do. Sometimes all the guidance we had was to just worship and let the point person see what God did in the moment. Other times, we may be led to pre-assign prayer teams whom youth could approach for prayers for Holy Spirit empowerment, spiritual gifts, or personal needs.

One night that I will not soon forget was Friday night because that Friday night was God's Grand Finale. Friday was a much-anticipated day. After the morning teaching, we were scheduled to go out on Friday afternoon to do outreach in Black Mountain. This is always a stretching and often delightful experience for most involved.

Outreach went well, in part because we had a great group of youth who were willing to take risks. The youth had an opportunity to practice listening to the Lord's guidance regarding where to go, whom to talk to or pray for, and in some cases, were able to share the gospel. I was thankful for all the stories I heard. Yet God had more. He had a surprise waiting for us that I had not anticipated.

Prior to the evening session the leaders met to discern God's plan for the evening. It was clear we would need to give some space for worship and testimony time from the afternoon outreach. But, what did God want to do after that? As our leadership team waited on God, what came to my mind was a Quaker-style prayer meeting where everyone sits in a circle and waits on the Lord for how to bless others. The Scripture that goes with this activity is:

> *"What then shall we say, brothers and sisters? When you come together, each of you has a hymn, or a word of instruction, a revelation, a tongue or an interpretation. Everything must be done so that the church may be built up,"* 1 Corinthians 14:26, NIV.

The guidance for this style of prayer meeting was a surprise to me, especially after our intense afternoon of outreach. Yet, when I shared my sense with the others in leadership, they agreed. A few hours later it became a reality.

We sat in a circle and watched God move. Wow! One person after another received words of encouragement and prophecy. Often there were multiple confirming witnesses from others. It wasn't just "leaders" giving words either. Rather these youth were participating as leaders themselves, even giving words to the older leaders. The Holy Spirit was powerfully present with us.

At 9:45, I looked at the two camp directors who seemed tired. We were trying to discern how long to let things go on. I must admit, I think we let our physical tiredness cloud the discernment at one point. I started to say that we would be wrapping up soon, but one of the students objected and wanted to share more. We all realized the Holy Spirit was not done and we best let Him continue! And continue He did! It was closer to 10:30p when we finally finished. He also provided some much-needed words for those of us in leadership, too!

Just imagine with me: Following tiring week of camp, youth (and adults) sat in a circle for nearly 2.5 hours. Though physically tired, all were engaged. God spoke through nearly everyone … powerfully! No one seemed bored or really even restless. This to me was miraculous. Anyone who says youth today aren't interested in God needs to broaden their horizons a bit because when God is the leader, He sure keeps it interesting!

I praise God for this "gift ending" to Upward Challenge 2018. It was God's Grand Finale for us. Not only did He bless everyone present; He also orchestrated a completely reproducible model for ministry anywhere two or three are gathered in Jesus name. My prayer is that each brother and sister who experienced that night is able to have similar prayer meetings in their home town, and the joy of the Lord spreads. I pray that also for you as you read this testimony. Upward Challenge 2018 is over, but God has more in store for us all. Praise the Lord!

3. A desire to witness.

> *You will receive power when the Holy Spirit has come upon you, <u>and you will be my witnesses</u> in Jerusalem and in all Judea and Samaria, and to the end of the earth.* Acts 1:8, ESV

4. A desire for fruit of the Spirit to grow and develop in their lives and the lives of others.

> *The fruit of the Spirit is love, joy, peace, patience, kindness, goodness, faithfulness, gentleness, self-control; against such things there is no law.* Galatians 5:22-23, ESV

Let's become who we already are, charismatic!

6. Getting to Know the Holy Spirit

Many times I begin the day by saying, "Good morning Father, Son, and Holy Spirit." Our Triune God is helping me to develop a deeper relationship with Himself, including that often-neglected member, the Holy Spirit.

A. Who the Holy Spirit Is

I was surprised to learn that a high percentage of younger adults in our day do not believe that the Holy Spirit is a Person. In total, observed the Barna Group,

> 68% of Mosaic Christians said they believe that the third person of the Trinity is just "a symbol of God's power or presence, but is not a living entity." This compares to 59% of Busters, 55% of Boomers, and 56% of Elders who believe the Holy Spirit is merely symbolic.[49]

In contrast, Scripture's consistent and clear witness is this: The Holy Spirit is a Person with whom we may have a personal relationship.

---

[49] The Barna Group. "How Different Generations View and Engage with Charismatic and Pentecostal Christianity." https://www.barna.org. March 29, 2010

	The Holy Spirit is ...
1	God. *... to <u>lie to the Holy Spirit</u> ... You have not <u>lied</u> to man but <u>to God</u>.* Acts 5:3-4, ESV
2	Eternal. *... how much more will the blood of Christ, who through <u>the eternal Spirit</u> offered himself without blemish to God,* Hebrews 9:14, ESV
3	Sovereign . *"The wind blows wherever it pleases."* John 3:8, NIV
4	Holy. *... was declared to be the Son of God in power according to the <u>Spirit of holiness</u>,* Romans 1:4, ESV
5	One, not many. *There is one body and <u>one Spirit</u>,* Ephesians 4:4, ESV
6	Our eternal Helper who speaks truth. *I will ask the Father, and he will give you another <u>Helper</u>, to be with you forever, even the <u>Spirit of truth</u>,* John 14:16-17, ESV
7	Omnipresent: Everywhere present. *Where shall I go from your Spirit? Or where shall I flee from your presence?* Psalm 139:7, ESV
8	Omnipotent: All powerful. *The Holy Spirit will come upon you, and the power of the Most High will overshadow you,* Luke 1:35, ESV
9	Omniscient: All knowing. *The Spirit searches everything, even the depths of God.* 1 Corinthians 2:10, ESV

10	The Holy Spirit is a Person who may be grieved. *And do not grieve the Holy Spirit of God,* Ephesians 4:30, ESV
11	The Holy Spirit is a leader who may be resisted. *You stiff-necked people, uncircumcised in heart and ears, you always resist the Holy Spirit.* Acts 7:51, ESV
12	The Holy Spirit is a Person whose power may be quenched. *Do not quench the Spirit.* 1 Thessalonians 5:19, ESV
13	The Holy Spirit is a Person with whom we may enjoy sweet fellowship. *The grace of the Lord Jesus Christ and the love of God and the fellowship of the Holy Spirit be with you all.* 1 Corinthians 13:14, ESV

So what?

Implications that flow from the above observations include the following:

1. Since He is God, the Holy Spirit, like the Father and the Son, is worthy of our worship.

2. Since the Holy Spirit is a Person, we can develop and enjoy an ever-deepening personal relationship with Him just as we can with the Father and the Son.

Even though I have believed for years that the Holy Spirit is a Person, only recently have I begun to cultivate a personal relationship with Him. Because of who He is and what He does, I am finding that the rewards are well worth the effort.

Illustration: Growing in Intimacy with God the Father, Son, and Holy Spirit
By Tamera Brockman

Today I [Tamera] spend some time sitting and listening to some music that helps me focus on God's love for me. I try to remove all agendas from my mind, not thinking of asking God to solve any problems, just trying to spend some time with Him. It does not take long (just a few minutes) before the Holy Spirit is revealing pictures in my sanctified imagination.

I see a picture of angels at my feet in front of where I am sitting on the couch. The message of what is happening which the Holy Spirit is communicating to my imagination and my spirit is that the angels are preparing my feet for the path ahead, for my destiny.

Another heavenly picture that the Holy Spirit is revealing in my imagination is a picture of me playing catch with Father God in heaven. Father God is comforting me about His love and guiding my aim in heaven so that it will not miss the mark like it does on earth. The Holy Spirit is also allowing me to see that when I throw the ball to Father God, love and blessings are flying off the ball and landing on me and in my ears!

B. The Holy Spirit Dwells <u>In</u> Every True Believer.

This is important. At the moment we are born again, the Holy Spirit comes to dwell <u>within</u> us. A series of statements in Scripture make this plain.

> ... and hope does not put us to shame, because God's love has been poured into our hearts through the Holy Spirit who <u>has been given to us</u>. Romans 5:5, ESV

> You, however, are not in the flesh but in the Spirit, if in fact the Spirit of God dwells <u>in</u> you. Anyone who does not have the Spirit of Christ does not belong to him. Romans 8:9, ESV

> *By one Spirit we were all baptized into one body, whether Jews or Greeks, whether slaves or free, and we were <u>all made to drink of one Spirit</u>. 1 Corinthians 12:13, NAS*[50]

The point is this: if you are a Christian, you already have the Holy Spirit dwelling <u>within</u> you. He is working deep in you to transform you into Christ-likeness by growing the fruit of the Spirit in your life. This good news includes the reality that

> *He who began a good work in you will bring it to completion at the day of Jesus Christ. Philippians 1:6, ESV*[51]

God is committed to our complete sanctification (see 1 Thessalonians 5:23-24).

---

[50] See also John 14:16-17 and Galatians 3:2, 4:6.
[51] Paul sounds a similar, triumphant note in 1 Thessalonians 5:23-24.

C. Inward and Outward Works of the Holy Spirit

The INWARD work of the Holy Spirit The Holy Spirit WITHIN	The OUTWARD work of the Holy Spirit The Holy Spirit UPON
✓ At conversion He regenerates us giving us new life ✓ Permanently dwells within us working to transform us from the inside out ✓ For our sanctification and holiness; for character development. ✓ Deepens our communion with, and our intimacy with, God ✓ Grows the Fruit of the Spirit in us	✓ After conversion ✓ Periodic; episodic; occurs on an "as needed" basis ✓ Releases power. Empowers us for dynamic action (witness; ministry; service) ✓ Activates and releases the manifestations of the Holy Spirit for the common good (1 Corinthians 12:7f.)

- The inward work of the Holy Spirit produces character transformation within us.

- The outward work of the Holy Spirit – His empowering work – blesses and builds up others, producing changes in them and/or in their circumstances.

- Jesus desires that we grow in both the inward and outward works of the Holy Spirit – transformation and empowerment.

To say it another way:

Conversion	Baptism with the Holy Spirit
Regeneration Sanctification Inward-focused power conforming us to the image of Christ. Includes the Romans 12 spiritual gifts, a.k.a., the "<u>functional gifts</u>" of the Spirit.	Adds dynamic, outward-focused power for witness and service (Acts 1:8) Removes barriers that held back the <u>manifestations of the Spirit</u> for the common good (1 Corinthians 12:7-11). Unlocks and expands a capacity; Activates a potential; Adds greater power.

D. Hinge Events

"Hinge events" are turning points. Before the hinge event, life was one way; after, things are significantly different. As we press-in to know Jesus, He strategically places hinge events in our lives. In the New Testament, Jesus' baptism was a hinge event in His life, and Pentecost was a hinge event for Jesus' disciples.

	Before	After
<u>Jesus' baptism</u> with the Holy Spirit	No teaching.[52] No miracles. No casting out evil spirits.	Jesus ministered dynamically in the Spirit's power to resist temptation, teach, preach, heal, cast our evil spirits, and make disciples.
<u>Pentecost</u>, the Apostles' and disciples' baptism with the Holy Spirit	Following Jesus' resurrection and prior to Pentecost, there is no record of the Apostles engaging in any ministry activities. They tarried in prayer in Jerusalem, waiting like seeds in the soil to be quickened, and like sails on the sea to be filled with wind.	The Holy Spirit quickened the seed and He filled their sails. The Holy Spirit dynamically empowered them to advance the gospel. He enabled them to speak anointed words and perform mighty works (signs and wonders) that verified that their message was true and pointed people to Jesus.
<u>Our baptism with the Holy Spirit</u> (our personal Pentecost)	Before …	After …

---

[52] His interactions with elders in Luke 2:46-47 may have included some teaching.

- Just as Jesus' baptism with the Holy Spirit was a hinge event in His life,
- and just as the Apostle's baptism with the Holy Spirit on the Day of Pentecost was a hinge event in their lives,
- so our "personal Pentecost," our baptism with the Holy Spirit, will be a hinge event in our lives.

E. What the Holy Spirit Does

Throughout our lives the Holy Spirit is working.

Pre-conversion works of the Holy Spirit

		The Holy Spirit ...
1	1 Peter 1:1-2 John 6:44	Sanctifies us in the sense that He sets us apart for salvation and draws us toward Jesus. Some call this "prevenient grace;"[53] others, "common grace."
2	John 16:7-8 Acts 2:37	Convicts of sin, righteousness, and judgment.

---

[53] The term prevenient comes from a Latin word that means "to come before, to anticipate." Prevenient grace is a phrase used to describe the grace given by God that precedes the act of a sinner exercising saving faith in Jesus Christ. https://www.gotquestions.org/prevenient-grace.html

Conversion: The Holy Spirit's Role

		The Holy Spirit …
1	John 3:5-8 John 6:63 Titus 3:4-7	The Holy Spirit washes, regenerates, and renews those who are appointed to salvation. By grace He justifies them and gives them eternal life.
2	John 20:22; John 14:16-17; Romans 8:9; 1 Corinthians 6:19; 12:13c	Comes to live IN us.
3	Romans 8:15-16	Adopts us into our Heavenly Father's family and bears witness that we are God's children.
4	2 Corinthians 1:21	Seals our salvation.
5	1 Cor. 12:13	Baptizes us into [plunges us into] the body of Christ.[54]

Post-Conversion works of the Holy Spirit

		The Holy Spirit …
1	Philippians 3:3 John 4:23-24	Helps us worship Jesus.
2	John 14:16-17 Romans 8:9	Dwells in us and is with us. Companionship, friendship. Dwells in every true believer. Cf. Acts 5:32
3	John 14:25-26	The Holy Spirit is our helper. He helps us through life.

---

[54] Since the interpretation of this key text is debated, I will explain my view under the heading, "1 Corinthians 12:13: Meaning?"

	John 15:26-27 John 16:7-15	The Holy Spirit is our teacher. He teaches us truth. The Holy Spirit bears witness to Jesus, i.e., He points our attention to Jesus. He glorifies Jesus. Cf. John 16:14; 15:27 The Holy Spirit convicts us of sin, righteousness, and judgment. The Holy Spirit is the Spirit of truth. He is true and speaks truth. The Holy Spirit guides us into all truth.
4	Acts 5:32 1 Corinthians 2:7-13	The Holy Spirit knows the Father's thoughts. The Father reveals His thoughts to us through the Holy Spirit. The Holy Spirit communicates the Father's mind, heart, and will to us.
5	Acts 11:27-30	The Holy Spirit predicts the future; He releases prophetic words.
6	Acts 8:29 Acts 11:12 Acts 13:1-4 Ephesians 4:30	The Holy Spirit gives guidance. He speaks, communicates, and instructs.

7	Acts 16:6-10	The Holy Spirit is able to forbid, prevent, hinder, and hold back.
8	1 Corinthians 12:11	The Holy Spirit manifests His presence.
9	Romans 8:26-27	The Holy Spirit not only helps us pray, He also intercedes (prays) for us.
10	Romans 8:12-17	The Holy Spirit enables us put to death the deeds of the body. The Holy Spirit leads believers; He gives guidance. The Holy Spirit assures us that we are children of God.
11	Galatians 5:22-23 2 Cor. 3:17-18	He grows Christ-like character qualities (fruit) within us, transforming us from the inside out.
12	Acts 4:31	He fills places and spaces.
13	Romans 8:11	He will give life to our mortal bodies.
14	Acts 1:8	The Holy Spirit **empowers** us to witness and serve.

Illustration: The Holy Spirit Gives Guidance

Journal Entry, October 11, 2017, Clovis, CA

For several months I [Phil] have thought about serving in some
capacity at Fresno Pacific Biblical Seminary after I retire from
my position as Senior Pastor of the Chinese Community
Church in San Diego. We already purchased a home in the
Fresno/Clovis area in order to be closer to our kids and
grandkids. This week I took a few days off to travel to Clovis
in order to spend time with the family and work on projects in
our new home.

After having lunch with our son, Aaron, I went to Home Depot.
After purchasing the items I needed, I went to my car, turned
the key, and the radio came on, tuned to a Christian station.
The first thing I heard was an advertisement for the seminary.
Up to that point I had not been thinking about the seminary;
rather, I was totally focused on my project. However, at that
moment I distinctly "heard" the Holy Spirit whisper, "Go to the
Seminary." "This is crazy," I thought. "I have no appointment.
I've never been on campus. In fact, I don't even know where it
is. I'm wearing tennis shoes with paint on them and dirty work
clothes with holes in them. I haven't shaved in two days. I look
like a bum."

Following a brief internal struggle, I pulled out my phone and
searched for the Seminary. It was 15 minutes southwest. As I
began to drive, I felt like I was on a treasure hunt following the
Holy Spirit's clues.

When I approached campus, my GPS seemed confused. Right
turn, then left turn, then more left turns. Eventually I thought,
"I will park at the next spot I see." I parked and walked toward
a set of buildings. "Where is the seminary," I asked a lady who
was approaching me on the sidewalk. "Right there," she said,
pointing to a stately, old, two-story mansion that was merely
100 feet from where we were standing.

I climbed the steps, went into the "seminary house," and introduced myself to the receptionist. "I'm a retiring pastor," I said. "My wife and I are moving to this area and I'm wondering if the seminary has any needs that I can help with." After asking a few questions, she said, "Just a minute," and climbed up the beautiful winding staircase in the center of the house. A few minutes later a man came down and introduced himself. "I'm Terry," he said. I followed him to his office and learned that he was, in fact, the president of the seminary!

We spent about 20 minutes together. My appearance seemed to matter very little to him. He asked about my background and I asked about needs at the seminary. I also told him about my experience of the Holy Spirit's nudge in the Home Depot parking lot. Due to his personal background and training in Ignatian spirituality, he was keenly interested in that piece of the story. "I'm learning to pay attention to things like this," he said. Regarding the seminary, he commented, "Contrary to trends across the USA, we are growing. Unofficially, I have a couple of part-time positions I am thinking about filling." He outlined a position that sounded to me like a "spiritual director" role on one of their campuses, and he also talked about a need for a grant writer. My heart leaped with joy! After also sharing a little about my wife's background, he asked me to send both resumes. We prayed and parted ways.

Regardless of the outcome of this conversation, I stand amazed at the Holy Spirit's timing and guidance. He is up to something!

Illustration: Don't Out-Talk the Anointing

Wednesday morning, March 14, 2018
Black Mtn, NC. Community of the Cross.
Summit on "Growing the Church in the Power of the Holy Spirit." Approximately 20 were in attendance.

During a break time, Mary Ellen approached a few of us and said, "Dave Westra is struggling with some health issues and we need to pray for him before our meeting begins." Six of us sat in a circle and Dave shared briefly his situation. "A year ago, I was on sabbatical enjoying a little time in God's great creation with my family in Arizona. I developed chills, a cough, a fever, headaches, and felt very weak. After twelve days, my family took me to the ER in Phoenix where I was diagnosed with a viral infection, pneumonia, complications from the pneumonia, and another infection, which was later diagnosed as Valley Fever. I was on bedrest for most of our time in Arizona, finally regaining strength the week before our family was to return to Michigan. However, eight months later, my symptoms began to re-appear. Returning to my regular doctor I was treated for another case of pneumonia, but not all of my symptoms cleared up—I still have headaches, occasional chills, and feel weak. Nevertheless, in the midst of it all, Jesus has been awakening me an hour and a half early most mornings, taking me to Scripture, and teaching me about the Kingdom of God."

As I [Phil] listened to Dave, my first thought was, "Let's pray for healing." However, within a few seconds after going to prayer, the distinct thought came to mind, "We are looking at a man who is normally very strong but now is weak." Then I "heard," "My grace is sufficient for you, my strength is made perfect in weakness." Initially, I resisted sharing that thought because it did not align within my mindset, namely, that we were there to pray for Dave's healing. However, I am learning to share what God gives, not more, not less, not modified. As a wise mentor once told me, "Don't out-talk the anointing." Hence, I shared with Dave and the group what I had "heard." Somewhat to my surprise, others had heard similar themes. Dave beamed and said, "During this season God is giving me real joy in the midst of my weaknesses."

I believe that in His time God will completely heal Dave. For now, God is teaching him lessons that can only be learned in the midst of physical weakness. Dave is submitting, relying on God in deeper ways, and growing stronger in his spirit.

7. Signs and Wonders in the Early Church

"Empowerment" is one slice of a much bigger pie. The Holy Spirit not only convicts, regenerates, adopts, seals, teaches, intercedes, guides, and sanctifies; He also empowers Christians for witness and service (Acts 1:8). Following our "personal Pentecost," the Holy Spirit equips and releases us to be vessels through whom Jesus may perform signs and wonders.

Following Pentecost, signs and wonders occurred regularly in the early Church.

1) Through Peter, in Jerusalem. Acts 3:1-10
2) Through the Apostles, in Jerusalem. Acts 5:12-16
3) Through Philip, in Samaria. Acts 8:4-8
4) Through Paul, in the city of Paphos on the Island of Cyprus. Acts 13:8-12
5) Through Paul, in the city of Lystra. Acts 14:8-10
6) Through Paul, in Ephesus. Acts 19:11-20

Signs and wonders occurred in every phase of the early church's expansion. God used them as a means to the end of advancing the gospel.

Implication:

In many cases Jesus intends to advance the gospel in our communities and world by using a similar strategy: preaching the gospel *plus* signs and wonders. We will say more about this important dynamic in the chapter entitled, "Word *and* Power Churches."

8. Passing on the Anointing

In the Book of Acts most major advances of the gospel included both conversion and empowerment. The Mother Church, specifically, the Jerusalem Apostles and/or their representatives, visited new church plants in order to inspect and legitimatize them. The Apostles consistently included an impartation of the grace of empowerment.

	The Jerusalem Church's Action	Outcome
Samaria Acts 8:14-17	Acts 8:14 Sent Peter and John to Samaria.	*Then they laid their hands on them and they received[55] the Holy Spirit. Acts 8:17, ESV*
Caesarea, Cornelius Acts 10-11	No additional action needed by the Jerusalem Church because Peter was already there.	*For they were hearing them speaking in tongues and extolling God. Then Peter declared, "Can anyone withhold water for baptizing these people, who have received the Holy Spirit just as we have?" Acts 10:46-47, ESV*
Antioch Acts 11:19-26	Sent Barnabas to Antioch, Acts 11:22	Many new converts. No mention of empowerment.
Ephesus Acts 19:1-7	None, because by this time, Paul was viewed as an official Church leader.	a) Baptized in the name of Jesus (19:5). = their conversion. b) Paul laid his hands on them and the Holy Spirit came on them (19:6). = their empowerment.

Paul's summary statement to the Jerusalem Council included both themes - salvation and empowerment:

---

[55] In one of the next chapters we will elaborate on the dual meaning of "received." Here, it means received for empowerment.

> *God, who knows the heart, bore witness to them, by giving them the Holy Spirit just as he did to us, and he made no distinction between us and them, having cleansed their hearts by faith. Acts 15:8-9, ESV*

At the Chinese Community Church, where I had the honor of serving as senior pastor for 12 years, when we baptized people in water we placed them under the water and raised them up again, thereby celebrating their spiritual union with Christ in His death and resurrection. While the person was still standing in the baptismal tub – which was originally designed to be a watering tank for cattle! – the Pastor(s) along a few others laid hands on him or her and called on Jesus to baptize them with the Holy Spirit, that is, to send His Holy Spirit upon them releasing their spiritual gifts and equipping them for effective witness and service.

Recently I learned that this practice dates back to the early Church. For example, Tertullian, writing near the close of the second century, in his book on *Baptism*, Chapter vi, said:

> The baptized when they come up out of the bath, are anointed with the holy oil, and then the hand is laid upon them with the invocation of the Holy Spirit.[56]

9. Going Deeper

In this section I will address a few issues that have caused confusion and division within some Christian circles. Getting a balanced perspective on these will lead toward greater understanding, unity, freedom, joy, and fruitfulness. I suggest

---

[56] James Gilchrist Lawson, *Deeper Experiences of Famous Christians* (Anderson, IN: Warner Press, Inc., 1911, Second Printing, July 1972), 42.

that you skim through this section and then return to linger on topics that interest you at this time.

A. 1 Corinthians 12:13: Meaning?

> *For by one Spirit we were all baptized into one body, whether Jews or Greeks, whether slaves or free, and we were all made to drink of one Spirit. 1 Corinthians 12:13, NAS*

As we noted above, John Stott used this verse as a proof text for his belief that every Christian is baptized with the Holy Spirit at the time of their conversion. Hence, it is unnecessary for believers to seek a baptism with the Holy Spirit.

However, is that what the Apostle Paul is really saying in 1 Corinthians 12:13? I think not.

A key question is this: Who does the baptizing? and, What is the result? My firm conclusion regarding 1 Corinthians 12:13 is that the NAS translation is correct. The NAS identifies the Holy Spirit as the baptizer and this baptism plunges converts to Christianity into the Body of Christ, the Church. 1 Corinthians 12:13 is not a reference to baptism with the Holy Spirit but baptism by the Holy Spirit. By comparison, texts such as Matthew 3:11, John 1:33, and Acts 1:5 declare that Jesus is the One who baptizes us with the Holy Spirit.

B. Paul Did Not Use This Phrase. Why?

The Apostle Paul did not use the phrase "baptism with the Holy Spirit." Why not?

The short answer is, "I don't know." However, three things are undeniably true.

   1. On three occasions, Dr. Luke recorded Paul's

conversion experience (Acts 9:1-22; 22:1-16; 26:12-23) and in the first of the three, Paul alluded to his baptism with the Holy Spirit. Specifically, in Acts 9:17-18, Ananias laid his hands on Saul/Paul and said,

> *"Brother Saul, the Lord Jesus who appeared to you on the road by which you came has sent me so that you may regain your sight and be filled[57] with the Holy Spirit."* (ESV)

2. Following his conversion, Paul ministered in the Spirit's power.

   Example:

   - *"God was doing extraordinary miracles by the hands of Paul, so that even handkerchiefs or aprons that had touched his skin were carried away to the sick, and their diseases left them and the evil spirits came out of them."* *Acts 19:11-12, ESV*

3. Paul believed that it was important to pray for people to receive the Holy Spirit so that they, too, would be better equipped to fulfill our mandate in Acts 1:8.

   Example:
   - As soon as the twelve men whom Paul met in Ephesus became Christians (Acts 19:5), *"Paul had laid his hands on them, the Holy Spirit came on them, and they began speaking in tongues and prophesying."* *Acts 19:6, ESV*

---

[57] Greek: pim-play-me, for short-term filling. See this chapter, Part D, "The Dual Meaning of 'Filled.'"

Nevertheless, in his thirteen letters, Paul did not insist that the believers to whom he was writing be baptized with the Holy Spirit, nor did he urge them to pass on this grace of empowerment to the people who would came to Christ through their witness.

Permit me to suggest two reasons why.

A. Paul saw no need to repeat the teachings on this subject already recorded in the Gospel of Luke and the Book of Acts.

B. Empowerment is only one dimension of a well-round Christian's walk. Paul concentrated on his audience's current needs such as:

- Solid doctrine about Jesus' life, death, and resurrection
- A clear understanding of justification and sanctification
- Healthy relationships
- Christ-like character qualities
- Holding onto hope
- Resisting our adversary

C. The Dual Meaning of "Received"

Received … meaning saved, converted, regenerated	Received … meaning empowered
12 But when they <u>*believed*</u> *Philip as he preached good news about the kingdom of God and the name of Jesus Christ, they were baptized, both men and women. 13 Even Simon himself* <u>*believed*</u>*, and after being baptized he continued with Philip.* *And seeing signs and great miracles performed, he was amazed.* *14 Now when the apostles at Jerusalem heard that Samaria had* <u>*received the word of God*</u>*, they sent to them Peter and John, Acts 8:12-14, ESV*	*… who came down and prayed for them that they might* <u>*receive the Holy Spirit,*</u> *16 for he had not yet* <u>*fallen on*</u> *any of them, but they had only been baptized in the name of the Lord Jesus. 17 Then they laid their hands on them and they* <u>*received the Holy Spirit*</u>*.* *18 Now when Simon saw that the Spirit was given through the laying on of the apostles' hands …* *Acts 8:15-18, ESV*

See also:
    John 1:12
    Romans 8:15
    John 20:21-22
    Acts 2:38-41
    Acts 8:13-14
	Simon "saw" something, probably a manifestation of the Spirit such as speaking in tongues.

D. The Dual Meaning of "Filled"

Three different Greek words are translated by English words related to "filled." Understanding their distinctions in meaning sheds light on several texts related to the empowering work of the Holy Spirit.

play-ro-o and play-race	pim-play-me
Describes a state of being. Describes long-term filling for sanctification. Is not followed by dramatic action. Example: A tree is filled with sap. Pertains to: • Holy Spirit "within" for transformation • Filled with the Holy Spirit for Christ-like character development. • Produces Romans 12 spiritual gifts. Matthew 13:48 Luke 2:40 John 12:3 Acts 2:28 Acts 5:3 Acts 5:28 Romans 15:3	A temporary filling. Pertains to short-term filling with the Holy Spirit for power. • Episodic • Equips us to engage *kairos* moments • Leads to dynamic action. The Holy Spirit works powerfully through us (words and/or works) to advance Jesus' agenda for that person or situation. Then, He "lifts." • Produces 1 Corinthians 12:7-11 manifestations of the Spirit for the common good Luke 1:41-42 Luke 1:67 Acts 2:4 Acts 4:8 Acts 4:31

John 1:14 Luke 4:1 Ephesians 4:10 Ephesians 5:18 Colossians 2:9-10 Acts 2:2 Acts 6:3,5 Acts 7:55 Acts 11:24 Acts 13:52	Acts 9:17-18 Acts 13:9-10

E. Filled ... and Filled Again

In Acts 2:4, the Apostles and disciples were filled with the Holy Spirit. In the examples that follow, many of the same people who had been filled are filled again.

Acts 2:4	And *they were all filled with the Holy Spirit* *and began to speak in other tongues as the* *Spirit gave them utterance. Acts 2:4, ESV*
Acts 4:8	*Then Peter, filled with the Holy Spirit, said to* *them, "Rulers of the people and elders, 9 if we* *are being examined today concerning a good* *deed done to a crippled man, by what means* *this man has been healed ... Acts 4:8, ESV*
Acts 4:31	*And when they had prayed, the place in which* *they were gathered together was shaken,* *and they were all filled with the Holy Spirit* *and continued to speak the word of God with* *boldness. Acts 4:31, ESV*

These texts illustrate that the empowering work of the Holy Spirit is not continuous; rather, it is episodic. When Jesus has finished working through us to complete His agenda for a particular person or situation, the Spirit "lifts." When it is Jesus' time for our next assignment, He will send a fresh anointing of the Holy Spirit upon us.

Illustration

As we stood in worship today, I [Phil] silently and desperately prayed, "Lord, I'm not ready to teach. And, I am not sure that the message I've prepared will hit the mark." Shortly thereafter the Holy Spirit drew near and began ministering to my spirit by interceding for me ... in tongues. Quietly and intensely tongues flowed. No one around me knew was going on, but I sensed that God was preparing me for the work He wanted to do through me that morning. A few minutes later the ministry of the Spirit that was bathing my spirit subsided and it was time to stand and teach. The Lord gave amazing freedom, passion, and clarity, and, based on responses following the service, the message hit the mark. All gory to Jesus.

10. *"Word and Power"* Churches

"Word *and* power" churches are churches

- ... where signs and wonders create opportunities to preach the gospel; and/or,

- ... where the preaching of the gospel is confirmed by signs and wonders.

Here is an illustration by Brenda Salter McNeil.

I once met a brother from Ghana, West Africa, who was completing his PhD in the School of World Missions at Fuller Theological Seminary. During one of his trips home, he attempted to share the gospel with several people who lived in his community. Although they listened respectfully, no one turned to Jesus Christ. He later learned that they were intimidated by a witch doctor who lived nearby. The witch doctor kept a symbol of his authority hanging outside his home: a lattice basket, filled with water, that never leaked. My friend decided to pray that God would empty the basket.

He stayed outside the home of the witch doctor and prayed all night that God would demonstrate his power. At some point he fell asleep. The next morning he was awakened by a commotion. The basket was empty. That town saw a mass revival as people learned about the God who caused the water to come out of the basket. There had been a power encounter—and God had won.[58]

In the Book of Acts, the marriage of "word" *and* "power" produced world-changing results. Here are a few examples.

	Signs and Wonders	Gospel Preached	Outcome
Pentecost	Heard their language, Acts 2:1-13	Peter preached, Acts 2:14-41	3000 converted, Acts 2:41
On the way to the temple	Beggar healed, Acts 3:1-10	Peter preached, Acts 3:11-26	~5000 believed, Acts 4:4

[58] Brenda Salter McNeil, "Behold, the Global Church," (Christianity Today: November, 2006), 45.

	Signs and Wonders	Gospel Preached	Outcome
Caesarea	Cornelius saw a vision, Acts 10:1-8	Peter preached, Acts 10:34-43	All who heard believed and were baptized with the Spirit. Acts 10:44-48
Lystra	Paul healed a cripple, Acts 14:7-10	Paul preached, Acts 14:11-18	None mentioned

In the following examples the order is reversed.

	Gospel preached	Signs and Wonders	Outcome
Philip, Samaria	Philip preached, Acts 8:4-5	Signs and wonders followed, Acts 8:6-8	Much joy in that city, Acts 8:8
Iconium	Paul and Barnabas spoke, Acts 14:1-3	Signs and wonders followed, Acts 14:3	Jews and Greeks believed, Acts 14:1

Illustration: An Amazing Day of Downtown Evangelism!

By Jay Knoblock

My friend Donnie and I did a number of evangelistic outreaches in Rosa Parks Circle in downtown Grand Rapids, MI, on some Saturdays in 2013. I recall one Saturday where God especially anointed us with the power of the Holy Spirit.

Before going out that day, I had done some listening prayer for "clues" regarding whom to talk to. God had revealed to me that I was to pray for "one on crutches nearby" and that "board games will produce conversation." Towards the end of our evening, Donnie and I were talking with our friend Gary outside of the Lantern Coffee shop. I looked up and saw "the man on crutches nearby" across the street. I felt the power of God come on me and I walked in their direction. I was a bit more timid as I got closer, as the man was with two of his other friends talking on the street. At first, I walked past the guys, wondering how to approach them. Yet it was clear the Lord wanted me to talk to them, so I went up and was obedient.

I openly told "the one on crutches" and his friend what we were doing. Initially, they didn't seem interested. Yet one of his friends asked me what other clues I had on my list. When I shared about the board game clue, he seemed intrigued. Not wanting to be intrusive on their conversation, I told them we'd be waiting for them to finish up their conversation if they cared to come over for prayer across the street. After 5 minutes or so, two of them came across and joined us!

We were able to pray for healing for the leg of "the one on crutches nearby," but that wasn't all of it. While Gary continued to minister to him, Donnie and I did listening prayer and spoke prophetically into the man curious about board games.

I don't recall everything that we said. I know much of what we told him did not make much sense to me. Yet it sure seemed to click with him! He was a recent college graduate from a local university, and shared about his work in efforts to produce a movie on angels and demons. He was stuck in his efforts to produce the movie, and the solution we gave him through listening prayer was that he was to "know God better." He was a nominal, curious Christian.

The next day, I received a voice message stating, "I want what you have." When I called him back, we had a conversation and I ended up leading him to receive Jesus as His Savior on the phone. Praise the Lord! I pray He grows as a disciple.

Gary ended up running into the man on crutches a few weeks later on the street. While he was not instantly healed, apparently, his leg healed quicker than the doctors expected. All glory to our great God!

Please note that signs and wonders were not the only factor in the Book of Acts that led to new converts and church growth. Persecution also created opportunities to preach the gospel.

Examples:
- Acts 5:17-32. The apostles were brought before the Council and Peter preached.
- Acts 6:8 – 7:53. Stephen preached; then, he was stoned.

Let's adopt the early church's prayer as our own:

> *And now, Lord, look upon their threats and grant to your servants to continue to speak your word with all boldness, 30 while you stretch out your hand to heal, and signs and wonders are performed through the name of your holy servant Jesus." Acts 4:29-30, ESV*

11. Summation: Your Personal Pentecost

The flow of the Book of Acts leads toward an important
question: "Have you experienced your 'personal Pentecost?'"

1	Jesus' "Pentecost"	Jordan River	Mt. 3:13-17
2	Jewish Pentecost	Jerusalem	Acts 2:1-4
3	Samaritan's "Pentecost"	Samaria	Acts 8:4-25
4	Saul's "Pentecost"	Damascus Road	Acts 9:1-19
5	Gentile's "Pentecost"	Cornelius in Caesarea	Acts 10:1-48; 11:1-18
6	Ephesians' "Pentecost"	Ephesus	Acts 19:1-7
7	**Your personal "Pentecost"**		

When we are baptized with the Holy Spirit, i.e., when we
experience our "personal Pentecost," the Holy Spirit, who is
already in us, fills us (Acts 2:4). This burst of Divine energy
begins to bring healing in inner wounds as well as to break
down internal barriers that held Him back. Further, it begins to
release the Holy Spirit to manifest power gifts (1 Corinthians
12:7-11) through us to advance the gospel, build up the
Church, and establish outposts of the Kingdom of God.

Note again Jesus' example. Following His baptism with the
Holy Spirit (Matthew 3:16-17; Mark 1:9-11; Luke 3:21-22;
John 1:32-33) – not before it, but after it – Jesus began to
preach, teach, perform miracles, and cast out demons.

Note again the disciple's example. Following Pentecost, i.e.,
following their baptism with the Holy Spirit (Acts 2:1-4), the

disciple's ministries included anointed words and powerful works. Signs and wonders buttressed the gospel message.

Something similar may happen to us. Following our baptism with the Holy Spirit, we will be better equipped to join the "dance of cooperation" with the Father, Son, and Holy Spirit. Jesus will beckon us, we will step onto the dance floor, He will lead the dance, and the Holy Spirit will work through us to advance the Father's agenda.

Invite Jesus to baptize you with the Holy Spirit!

Don't leave home without it.

Let us press on together, under the Lordship of Jesus Christ and the authority of His Word to advance the gospel in the power of the Holy Spirit.

What an adventure!

12. Living Spirit-Filled

Paul Stokes teamed with Brad Long and Cindy Strickler to write *Growing the Church in the Power of the Holy Spirit*. Paul's life and ministry have been, and are being, dynamically shaped by the Holy Spirit.

A Life and Ministry Shaped by the Holy Spirit
By Paul Stokes
United Kingdom

THE CALL

My call to gospel ministry came in the summer of 1984. At that time I was working on a motorway construction site near Uxbridge as part of my Civil Engineering training, and had a profound and vivid visionary encounter with Jesus Christ whilst cycling home from work. The Holy Spirit opened my spiritual eyes and overwhelmed me with a vision of the desperate state of those who are not yet Christians. I saw great crowds of people walking thoughtlessly past Jesus, across a hilltop and over the edge of a cliff, falling into the flaming chasm below. As I looked the Spirit gave me a small taste of the Father's sorrow for those who ignore His Son and my heart was broken with a love for the lost. I was burdened with a deep desire to reach out to them with the saving news about Jesus.

I poured out my prayer in writing.

> They don't know who they're rejecting …I want to share you with them. Can't we stop them? Can't we run a little faster, try a little harder to catch up with them before it's too late? I feel so futile, useless, unable to move before they fall. I want to help. I want to save them all. Do they have to die? Do they have to burn? Is there nothing I can do?

Towards the end of my writing I had a sense that the Lord was also speaking to me and I put that, too, on paper. One part reads:

> …be brave, love truth, and I will help you win them.

Peter quoted Joel's prophecy: "God says, I will pour out my Spirit on all people. Your sons and daughters will prophesy, your young men will see visions, your old men will dream dreams." (Acts 2:17) This was my own experience as Jesus Christ baptized me with the Holy Spirit. The vision that I saw, and the prophetic words God spoke into my life, were an invitation to join in the dance of cooperation with the Spirit and play my part in the work that he purposed.

Shortly afterwards I began the interviewing process for training as a minister, taking practical steps of faith and obedience in response to the Lord's invitation. This passion for the lost and desire to hear and heed the Holy Spirit have motivated my own ministry and have shaped the church that I serve. I do not believe this is a call or gifting for personal evangelism but rather a call to enable Jesus' church to engage fruitfully in the task of evangelism in cooperation with the Holy Spirit.

A Surprising Discovery

In the summer of 2005 I visited a colleague in Pennsylvania and browsed the "Britain" entry in his New International Dictionary of Pentecostal and Charismatic Movements. I was surprised to discover that I had met, been taught by or ministered to by some of the key leaders in British charismatic renewal. I worshipped regularly with St John's Church of England, Harborne, Birmingham under the leadership of Rev Tom Walker. Rev David McInnes was a speaker and overseer for my university Christian Union in Aston. Rev Nicky Gumbel and Rev Sandy Millar had been influential teachers through books and personal teaching during the early years of my ministry. I had been present at the International Charismatic Consultation on World Evangelization held in Brighton in July 1991 and, together with several other URC (United Reformed Church) ministers and ordinands, was prayed for by Rev Peterson Sozi, founder of the First Presbyterian Church in Uganda.

This was a revelatory moment for me as I had not previously been aware of the many different people God had used to speak into my life, establishing theological, spiritual and experiential foundations. And alongside these prominent names I could add a host of other lesser known but equally significant individuals. Christ-centered evangelism, Biblical authority, and the Holy Spirit have been fundamental aspects of my nurture and ministry.

VISIONS AND ENCOUNTERS RELATING TO PLYMSTOCK UNITED CHURCH

There have been many experiences of the Holy Spirit at work in Plymstock United Church where I serve as Pastor. The significance of these visions is that each of them has shaped, or is shaping, the direction and focus for the church's life. Each of them is living evidence that God speaks through His Holy Spirit and, as we respond in obedience, so we remain centred in His will.

GUIDANCE THROUGH A PROPHETIC WORD

Restore the Warmth

In 1993, during my first year at Plymstock, we received a prophetic message via Ted Coford which the Elders and I discerned to be authentic. It read:

> You people of Plymstock love your warm comfortable houses. But you have neglected your central place of worship, my temple. It is cold and uninviting. Can't you see what is happening? You hope for a large harvest but have received a small one. And what you have gathered I have blown away with the wind. Make provision to restore the warmth in my temple and I the Lord will be with you.

In the subsequent years the church invested in its premises by replacing the central heating systems; installing double-glazing; replacing the seats; cladding the fascia; installing a kitchenette for hospitality; replacing the noticeboard; resurfacing the hall floors; redecorating internally; constructing a wheelchair-friendly emergency exit.

During the first decade we saw numbers continue to decline (from 64 to 50) as more people left than joined. In the next decade numbers almost doubled, rising to 97 in 2011. It would be simplistic to attribute numerical growth to property improvements – persistent evangelistic efforts, especially the Alpha Course and (more recently) Café Vision, have been vital factors. But it is certainly true to say that we laboured and gave in order to be faithful to the prophetic word, and that God has indeed been with us and has drawn others to himself as well.

GUIDANCE THROUGH VISIONS

Link the Buildings

In the late 1990s we were struggling with questions of how to improve the premises. The original church building (Whitfeld Hall) was a derelict eyesore and we needed extra room for our work with infants, children and youth. We called the church to prayer, and one particular vision was received by Doreen Brown at that time. The vision was a picture of the two remaining church buildings – the worship space and Norley Hall – being joined together by an extension at the front of the site. This had been part of the initial design long before Doreen joined the church but now it was shown to us as a visionary picture which gave direction for the future. Subsequently the derelict building was demolished and became an outdoor play area. Now plans – and most of the finances – are in place for extending and linking the premises during 2013. This is practical, obedient fulfilment of the vision that was given and the need for extra space that is experienced.

A Host of Youth

Work with children and young people has been part of the church's DNA since its foundation, with the initial buildings having to be extended to accommodate the growing Sunday School classes. In November 2001 a group from Plymstock attended a day conference at Trinity Church, Cheltenham. Whilst there, Caroline Mahon received a vivid vision of the front lawn of the church crowded with many, many young people. The following year she pioneered a new group (Solid Rock) for young people which ran for several years, but saw no significant numerical growth. The church began to discuss the possibility of engaging a trainee youth worker but was initially reluctant to pursue this route. In 2010 we launched Dynamic, an open youth club, and watched the numbers grow to around 40. The following year we engaged a trainee youth worker via SWYM, helped by mission grants from the URC Synod and the national URC Mission Fund. The work is already expanding to include a faith-nurturing group for young people, and it seems that we are beginning to see the fulfilment of the vision initially given to Caroline.

Spreading Fire from Heaven

During the late 1990s I received a vision of the Holy Spirit falling on Plymstock United Church like a column of fire. I had been walking around the community, praying, and the vision came unexpectedly as I came along Randwick Park Road. I saw a wide, 'solid' column of fire (similar to the images on the "Independence Day" film posters!) falling onto the church buildings and then spreading out from there into the community and beyond. I have shared this vision with the church at various times, believing that it is God's revelation for the whole fellowship.

We have seen the vision being partly fulfilled in the lives of some individuals, for instance in my own involvement with GEAR and the Dunamis Project, together with the participation of other people in Dunamis and with healing and renewal ministries in Plymouth, nationally and internationally, and with individuals within the church who have experienced the fire of the Spirit falling upon them (I was able to list about 20 people quite easily and there will be others too.) And yet it also seems that this vision still lingers, waiting to happen more fully. I do not know quite what that looks like in practice, but somehow what has actually been experienced here seems to be more like some individual flames falling and reaching a few rather than the broad and spreading image that I saw. There may well be more yet to come.

Warning of Spiritual Attack

The final vision was more of a warning than a promise. In November 2009 I returned from South Korea where I had been training leaders and teachers for the Dunamis Project, and went for a prayer-walk. From Burrow Hill I looked over the community, praying, and was surprised to see an image of several large, dark figures squatting around the church and poking it like children with sticks in a fire. In my spirit it was obvious that these were malevolent trouble-makers, and I became aware that they related to some key areas of the church's life and fellowship that were going to come under attack. These were: youth and children's work; relationships with one another; worship and music; and people's physical health. A fifth area had to do with a shoulder-shrugging indifference, apathy or defeatism. We experienced some of these in quite obvious ways in the year that followed, and I believe it would be naïve and careless to relegate this warning to the past.

VISIONS AND ENCOUNTERS RELATING TO DUNAMIS

As well as these local church focused visions there has been another series of spiritual encounters and visions which relate to my own walk with Jesus. These have continued and built

upon the initial vision which led to me training for the
Ministry.

My Call into Dunamis

In September 2001 we hosted a GEAR day conference at
Plymstock United Church. The "Romans 1:11 Trust" works to
provide a cross-fertilization of training and ministry resources
between the URC and some African churches and we had
arranged to have Rev Wilberforce Wabulo from Uganda and
Rev Colin Bones (a GEAR committee member from Poole) to
share testimony, teaching and prayer ministry. It was a well-
attended conference. Prayer was a major emphasis in the
teaching and Dunamis was advertised briefly. At the end of the
day I was satisfied that we had run a "successful" event and felt
quite pleased. But the impact ran deeper than I thought.
The following morning I found myself awakened and walking
the streets at 7.00 am, praying (this was most definitely not my
normal practice.) In the midst of that time of prayer I sensed
God speaking, telling me that I should attend Dunamis. I
disagreed and argued with Him!   As far as I could remember,
the dates clashed with several events already in the Church's
calendar and it would be difficult to rearrange them.
Nevertheless, the guidance seemed clear and eventually I
reluctantly agreed to see if it was possible. The timing clashed
with the need to chair a Church Members' AGM at Laira, an
Elders' Meeting for Plymstock, and on the Sunday we had
unchurched guests bringing their baby to Plymstock for a
blessing. To attend Dunamis I was going to have to disrupt
many people's schedules and, more significantly, cause
problems for a visiting family. But the sense of God's call just
wouldn't go away and so, after discussion with my wife and
with Elders from both churches, I made the necessary
rearrangements and booked my place for the November retreat.
This focused on prayer and was the third in a series of six
similar events. It was my introduction to the international
ministry that is Dunamis, and happened only because the Holy
Spirit had been very persistent in "cornering" me!

A Vision of Flying to America

In May 2002 I went to my second Dunamis event, "The Healing Ministry of Jesus," held in the Carey meeting room at the Wycliffe Centre in Buckinghamshire. In the midst of worship one evening, I found myself kneeling near the back of the room as others sang, and 'saw' a picture of myself seated on an airplane flying to America and knew it had something to do with Dunamis. I held onto it, choosing not to share it with others but rather to wait and see what God would do.

A month later the GEAR national chairman, Brian Harley, phoned inviting me to become part of the GEAR committee with special responsibility for continuing the Dunamis Project once the current cycle had been completed. I delayed answering for a day but knew clearly that my response needed to be "Yes". A few days later I received a transatlantic phone call from Brad Long. Brad is the Director of PRMI - the organization which administers the Dunamis Project internationally - and he had been the main teacher at the Dunamis retreats I had already attended. He spoke with great enthusiasm, delighted at my appointment, and then invited me to attend a meeting of the Dunamis Fellowship which would take place in North Carolina in August 2003. It was time to share the vision I had received and we both sensed clearly that here was God's calling and confirmation.

A year later I flew to America, sharing the journey with Rev Rob Pickering, and mid-Atlantic the image came back to mind, bringing with it a humbling sense of "Oh my goodness, I'm sat in the middle of that vision!"

Wrestling in Prayer on Sabbatical: Surrender

In the summer of 2007 I took a Sabbatical, and in June, I attended a week-long event at the Community of the Cross in Black Mountain, North Carolina, focused on Spiritual Leadership. Part way through the week we were invited to spend time in prayer surrendering ourselves and our ministries afresh to Jesus. As I knelt to pray I found myself able to place into God's hands my role at Pilgrim URC and my involvement with GEAR, willing to let go of these and walk away if He called me to do so. But then it came to the question of my ministry at Plymstock, and so began a wrestling match. I had a very strong sense of attachment and could not simply hand it back to God. I knew that this was wrong and surrendering was exactly what I needed to do, but for almost half an hour I struggled in prayer with a great many tears and clenched fists. All the while Joe Schlosser stood by me interceding, unaware of the details but very aware that the Holy Spirit had called him to stand with me at that time. After 25 minutes I found myself asking for permission to stay, and then realized that my fundamental attitude had shifted. Now I was speaking and praying as if it was Jesus' church and up to him whether or not I ministered there. Thankfully I had let go of the intense attachment.

And so I turned next to pray about my involvement with Dunamis. Deep inside I knew that this, too, was something I was not eager to let go of, and I feared that I was about to enter into another half-hour prayer wrestling match. But rather than a profound struggle, within a matter of moments I had a clear (almost anti-climactic!) sense of the Holy Spirit saying to me: "It's what I'm calling you to do." I therefore have a vividly clear sense of God's call to be part of the ministry of Dunamis.

With God Up a Mountain: Jesus' Call

On Saturday 20th June 2009, after the prototype conference for "Growing the Church in the Power of the Holy Spirit" I was alone and had the Community of the Cross to myself. I walked around the prayer trails, wanting to pray especially about leadership but also drawn into (or drifting off into?) other topics. I climbed the steep path up to Ascension Point and sat for a while in the rustic, wooden shelter overlooking tree-clad mountains. But then I felt drawn to stand in the sunshine at the edge of the log floor, eyes closed and hands held out in front of me, and so began another spiritual encounter.

I became aware of God placing into one hand a sceptre, symbolizing authority. Then into my other hand He placed a sword, symbolizing the Word of God. The stillness gave way to a steady rustling as the breeze blew through the trees around me and brought to mind Jesus' words comparing the Spirit with the wind and reminded me of both my various encounters with the Holy Spirit and also the teaching about co-operating with the Spirit which are the very heart of Dunamis. Then I heard Jesus saying to me: "Don't you leave this place until you are ready" (remember, I had been praying about leadership.) As I began to wonder just how long I would be stood there, he spoke again almost immediately, asking "So what are you still doing here?" In obedience I left that spot, assured that Jesus has indeed called and equipped me for leadership by giving authority (exousia) through Scripture and the empowered anointing (dunamis) of the Holy Spirit.

Sent to Korea

The autumn of 2009 saw me visit Jesus Abbey in Taebeck, South Korea, in order to provide training for some 60 pastors and leaders, equipping them for teaching and leading the Dunamis Project in that country. The invitation came just seven weeks beforehand when the planned teacher (Rev Tom Willcox) had to withdraw, and Rev Cindy Strickler made a phone call from Atlanta airport asking me to go in his stead. Jesus Abbey is the "womb" where the Dunamis Project was conceived and nurtured under the tutelage of Father Archer Torrey, grandson of R.A.Torrey, and I was overwhelmed by the opportunity to visit this spiritually significant venue as well as by the responsibility of providing training for other leaders. That phone call came on a Sunday afternoon. On the Monday I prayer walked in the local park and stood still in the dew-drenched grass wondering what to do. As I stepped away from that spot I sense God saying to me: "Don't you dare leave this spot until you've said 'Yes'." So I stepped back into my footmarks and eventually told him that, yes, I would go. I shared that request with the Elders (but not the prayer) and brought it before the church AGM on the Thursday, not wanting to go unless I had the blessing of the congregation.

Together we prayed, seeking revelation from the Holy Spirit, and two Elders both shared visions. One described a vision of me on a beach, with a host of Koreans running towards me round a headland, welcoming me with joy and enthusiasm. Another Elder (who had been very unconvinced) described a vision of me stood beside oriental hanging banners. Believing that this was the Lord's guidance, the church sent me on my way with its blessing.

Several other supernatural encounters could be added to this episode, for instance Annie Lewis receiving guidance about accompanying me as Intercessor, and someone being woken in the middle of the night as God spoke to them about giving to cover the cost of Annie's flight. Alongside these revelations and encounters, I was also struck by the fact that, of all the people involved in Dunamis worldwide, I was essentially the second choice teacher and leader. That in itself was humbling.

Overflowing Oil and Water

At the annual meeting of the Dunamis Fellowship in 2010, at the Wycliffe Centre, we were all asked to seek the Lord about how He was calling us to participate in the work of Dunamis. The Spirit prompted me to read Psalm 23, and many phrases seemed freshly relevant, most noticeably: "He makes me lie down in green pastures," and, "Even though I walk through the valley of the shadow of death, I will fear no evil." I was prompted to kneel and read aloud the latter verse (v4) as an affirmation of faith and trust especially in connection with whatever health issues I found myself facing (I awaiting medical tests at that time).

I then knew (through an impression in my mind) that I should go to the lawns around the conference centre and lie there (green pastures) …even though they were probably damp. The air was heavy – warm and moist – and the sun shining down on me. It was peaceful and a blessing in itself. Lying there I began to reflect prayerfully on my role in DFB&I and what area(s) seemed most "natural" to me. The main aspects that surfaced for focus were teacher-administrator and overseer, including 'teacher-teacher'.

Afterwards I knew I had to go to the main meeting room and ask whoever was there to anoint my head with oil. On leaving the grass I was prompted to pick up a small stick of wood, a symbolic promise-sign that God would accomplish His work in me. Graham Hill was available and faithfully anointed my head – plenty of oil – and prayed for me using imagery from Psalm 133:2. The first verse of that Psalm then dominated my thoughts with a focus on creating and maintaining the unity – the 'joined-togetherness' of this Dunamis Fellowship.
Finally I was prompted to take a cup, fill a jug with water, and go outside to pour the whole jugful into the cup so that it overflowed relentlessly, splashing round my feet. God has so much to pour out! And then I was instructed to drink the cupful, receiving and doing all that I was given by God – not part of it, but all of it (even though I wasn't particularly thirsty at the time!)

13. When No Breakthrough is in Sight

I share the following email because Brother Mark's experience may resonate with some of us.

February 2018
Good Morning Brother Phil,
My name is Mark (not his real name) and I came to know the Lord at a traditional Baptist church who does not believe in the baptism of the Holy Spirit, miracles or healing. I have a strange condition six years ago where I woke up one morning and could not walk. I then started going to the Pentecostal church for prayer and things manifested in my legs and feet but there was no healing or deliverance. In recent months I have felt spiritually dry and have begun praying and fasting for the baptism of the Holy Spirit as we read in Acts how it empowers us for life and ministry. I have not had a breakthrough yet and do not know what to do. What do you advise?
Thanks for your help and prayers.

Brother Mark

Dear Brother Mark,

I appreciate your honesty about your struggle. Unfortunately, I do not have a quick or easy answer for you because there are mysteries to the Christian life that are beyond me. I do know this: The Giver is more important than the gift. By this I mean that the value of a relationship with Jesus surpasses the value of His gifts of healing and baptism with the Holy Spirit. It seems that sometimes God tests our hearts by withholding what we long for. His test question for you may be, "Even if I never heal you, and even if you never experience the baptism with the Holy Spirit, will you still love me and serve me?"

May I also remind you that God is free. We cannot put Him in a box and we cannot manipulate Him into doing what we want done. He weighs motives and He will not share His glory with another.

One of my mentors, Brad Long, wrote a book that you might find helpful during this dry season in your life. It is called *Passage Through the Wilderness*. https://www.prmi.org/resources-from-prmi/books/passage-through-the-wilderness

As the Lord brings you to mind I will pray for you. May He draw you close to Himself and give you even more than the breakthroughs for which your heart longs.
His servant,
Phil

A Free Resource

Posted on PastorsPub.net you will find The *Holy Spirit Course* which emphasizes the empowering work of the Holy Spirit.

Bibliography

Bauer, Walter. Trananslated by William F. Arndt and F. Wilbur Gingrich (BAG). *A Greek-English Lexicon of the New Testament and Other Early Christain Literature.* Chicago, IL: The University of Chicago Press, Thirteenth Impression, 1971.

Bennett, Dennis and Rita. *The Holy Spirit and You.* Kingsway Publications, 1974.

ESVSB (English Standard Version Study Bible). Wheaton, IL: Crossway Bible, 2008.

Group, Barna. *How Different Generations View and Engage with Charismatic and Pentecostal Christianity.* https://www.barna.org, March 29, 2010.

Lawson, J. Gilchrist. *Deeper Experiences of Famous Christians.* Anderson, IN: The Warner Press, 1911; Second printing, July 1972.

Lawson, James Gilchrist. *Deeper Experiences of Famous Christians.* Anderson, IN: Warner Press, Inc., 1911, Second Printing, July 1972.

Long, Brad; McMurry, Douglas. *The Dunamis Project: Gateways to Empowered Ministry.* prmi.org, Revised 2006.

Long, Brad; Stokes, Paul K.; and Strickler, Cindy. *Growing the Church in the Power of the Holy Spirit: Seven Principles of Dynamic Cooperation.* Grand Rapids, MI: Zondervan, 2009.

Marshall, I. Howard. *The Acts of the Apostles.* Grand Rapids, MI: Eerdmans, Reprinted 1987.

Montague, George T. *The Holy Spirit: Growth of Biblical Tradition.* New York: Paulist Press, 1976.

Moreland, J. P. *Kingdom Triangle.* Grand Rapids, MI:
    Zondervan, 2007.

Noordmans, Philip J. *FireStarter: The Holy Spirit Empowers.*
    SolaKaleo Publishing, 2014.

R.C. Sproul, General Editor. *Reformation Study Bible.*
    Orlando, FL: Ligonier Ministries, 2005.

Stott, John. *God's New Society: The Message of Ephesians.*
    Downers Grove, IL: InterVarsity Press, 1980.

Whitaker, Bob. *Adventuring in the Spirit.* Lulu Publishing
    Services, 2015.

About the Author

I am a follower of Jesus Christ who has tasted the goodness of God and the powers of the age to come and hungers for more.

Since graduating from Fuller Theological Seminary in 1975, I have served in a variety of pastoral and teaching roles in the Midwest and California. In 1997, I received my D.Min. from Fuller. Hence, my formal title is Rev. Dr. Philip J. Noordmans.

Phil's Publications

1. *FireStarter: The Holy Spirit Empowers*

FireStarter mixes personal stories and careful exegesis to chronicle my journey from being a dispensational cessationist to living as a grateful, balanced charismatic. Check it out. Many people report that their understanding of the Person and work of the Holy Spirit has grown immensely as a result of reading this book. So have their experiences of His power and guidance. Life changing!

2. *Gleaning Meaning from God's Word: Better Bible Study Helps*

Is what that verse means to you what it really means?

Every student of Scripture and every teacher of Scripture will benefit from this easy to read introduction to hermeneutics, which is the art and science of interpreting Scripture. You will grow in your ability to accurately understand, apply, and teach the Word of Truth (2 Timothy 2:15). Better Bible study truly does help.

3. *Why Pray? Because Sometimes God Relents!*

In addition to wrestling with the meaning of "God relents," this booklet offers timeless insights into the mystery of prayer. As a result of this study my prayer life is being impacted for good. The illustrations will add courage to beleaguered pray-ers.

4. *The End: Charity Tracker and the Last Dance*

For years I have questioned the pre-tribulation rapture perspective behind publications such as the *Left Behind* series. This captivating novel builds on a wiser eschatological bedrock, one that encourages believers to anticipate and prepare for hard times ahead.

The appendices are worth their weight in gold in that they utilize bullet points and diagrams to summarize stepping stones to the end.

5. *A Primer on the Empowering Work of the Holy Spirit*

Utilizing a concise, readable format that includes numerous real-life stories, the author introduces those who hunger for more to the empowering work of the Holy Spirit. This *Primer* does not promote showmanship, sensationalism, or mindless faith; rather, it lays a solid, biblical foundation for a dynamic relationship with the Holy Spirit that is real, personal, and fulfilling, and that results in building healthy relationships and advancing the gospel.

Each of these books is **available on Amazon** as a paperback and eBook. Please be kind enough to leave a review on Amazon.

Teri and I enjoy life with our kids and grandkids. In my spare time I tend a small organic garden.

You may connect with me in the following ways:

- pnoordmans12@gmail.com
- PastorsPub.net

Soli Deo Gloria

Index

Made in the USA
Columbia, SC
06 February 2019